DIVORCE
RULES
FOR MEN

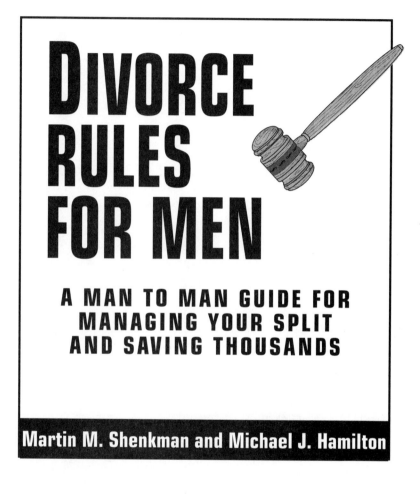

DIVORCE RULES FOR MEN

A MAN TO MAN GUIDE FOR MANAGING YOUR SPLIT AND SAVING THOUSANDS

Martin M. Shenkman and Michael J. Hamilton

JOHN WILEY & SONS, INC.

ACKNOWLEDGMENTS

We would like to thank the many experts who gave generously of their time and knowledge: Amy J. Amundsen of Memphis, TN; Colleen A. Brown, U.S. Bankruptcy Judge for the District of Vermont; Kenneth N. Condrell of Orchard Park, NY; Barry Croland of Shapiro & Croland in Hackensack, NJ; Paul Feinstein of Chicago, IL; Lynne Gold-Bikin of Wolf, Block, Schorr & Solis Cohen in Norristown, PA; Janet Andron Hoffman of Teaneck, NJ; Robert E. Holmes, Jr. of Holmes, Woods & Garza in Dallas, TX; Sidney Kess of New York City; David Leitman of Israel; David L. Levy of the Children's Rights Council in Washington, DC; Jonathan Pollack of Beldock, Levine & Hoffman in New York City; Lori Sackler of Sackler and Associates in New York City; Rob Schlegel of Houlihan Valuation Advisors in Indianapolis, IN; Saul M. Simon of Allmerica Financial in Edison, NJ; Lynne Strober of Mandelbaum, Salsburg, Gold, Lazris, Discenza & Steinberg in West Orange, NJ; Stanley Teitelbaum of Teaneck, NJ; Ginta Wall of San Diego, CA; Michele Weiner-Davis of Woodstock, IL; Bill Yegge of Wells, Maine; and Lydia Fogelman, editor of the *Matrimonial Strategist* for many years of encouragement and ideas. Any errors or mistakes are the authors.

Martin M. Shenkman
Michael J. Hamilton

New York City
June 1, 2000

CONTENTS

Contents

Contents

Contents

Contents

Contents

Contents

Contents

Contents

Contents

INTRODUCTION

WHAT THIS BOOK WILL DO FOR YOU

The statistics are startling: The United States has the highest divorce rate in the world. Divorce is a traumatic process for anyone unfortunate enough to have to go through it. It's difficult even for those who are only indirectly touched by it. Too frequently, the process gets out of control resulting in emotional and personal difficulties as well as significant financial costs. Knowing how to protect yourself and your assets, how to deal with the divorce process, and how to protect your parental rights can help reduce the inevitable stress.

Much of the information written for men on divorce takes the tone of warlike guerrilla tactics. While reading these may make you "feel good" if you're angry and want revenge, that approach is always counterproductive. This book provides *practical and useful information,* not vindictive war stories. It presents easy-to-read tips and pointers you may have missed or your advisers didn't tell you. It only takes a few workable ideas to make a world of difference, and this book offers more than 150 nuggets of advice.

We call the suggestions in this book "rules" because they are important in helping men survive the divorce process, from both a financial and a psychological/emotional point of view. But they are really just tips, ideas, suggestions, and recommendations, all intended to help you. Moreover, they are numbered simply for ease of reference: you don't need to follow them chronologically, and Rule 1 is not necessarily the most important thing you need to keep in mind. All the suggestions and ideas are equally important, and if you can use even just a few of them, your divorce process should be much easier on you, your children, and maybe even your ex-wife. And because "soon-to-be ex-wife" is a bit unwieldy, in this book we refer to her as your wife, your ex-wife, or your ex.

CAN YOU GIVE IT ONE MORE TRY

Financially, there are few things you can do in your life that are more ruinous than getting divorced. If you're reading this book, you probably have reached the point in your life where divorce seems the only option. But in view of the trauma divorce will bring to you and everyone you love, and even to those you once loved, take one last shot at saving your marriage. At least consider your other options before getting a lawyer.

THE "WALK-AWAY WIFE SYNDROME"

Close to 50 percent of marriages end in divorce and two-thirds of those divorce actions are filed by the wife—most often the "walk-away wife syndrome" is evident. Although unsuspecting husbands get the raw end of the deal on this one and often are in shock, but divorce is usually the result of a predictable pattern, notes Michele Weiner-Davis, author of *Divorce Busting* (Fireside

Books, 1993). In the early years of a marriage, the woman is often the caretaker of the relationship. If there isn't enough closeness or communication, the wife will pursue closeness. If the husband doesn't respond, she will usually complain about other things, such as money, not about the lack of intimacy. "I've never met a man who becomes closer to his wife from nagging," notes Weiner-Davis. So, the closeness that the women wants is never realized.

At some point, the woman realizes that nagging is nonproductive and she gives up. Years go by where the wife isn't pursuing closeness and isn't even nagging. The husband goes about his business, lulled into the status quo. Meanwhile, the wife decides for herself that she is leaving and develops an escape plan. It's different for each woman, but a typical plan is something like this: "When the youngest is off to college, I'm out of here."

More years go by, and one day the wife, according to plan, files for divorce. The husband is shocked, most of all because wives often file for reasons like "growing apart," not for infidelity or abuse. Although the wife thinks she's been verbalizing her unhappiness for years, her announcement that she wants a divorce, or is actually filing for one, is the first wake-up call most husbands hear to preserve their marriage. The sad part is that by this point the wife can't or won't make the effort to work out their problems. The wall between them, in the wife's view, is impervious. She wants out on the first occasion in the history of the marriage when she has her husband's attention.

CAN THE "LAST RESORT TECHNIQUE" SAVE YOUR MARRIAGE?

If your wife is on the way out, the "Last Resort Technique" may give you a final chance to save your marriage. Weiner-Davis explains how this technique works. The biggest problem to overcome is that when your wife is on her way out of your marriage, and you want to hold on to the relationship—when you feel something slipping through your fingers—your pursuit gets intense. You may get on a guilt trip, order flowers, buy little presents, purchase romantic greeting cards and leave them on the refrigerator, and constantly remind her of your presence. "One guy professed his love on a billboard," remembers Weiner-Davis. "Be careful in how you profess how wonderful a wife and mother she is," cautions Amy J. Amundsen, Esq., "it may hurt you later in the divorce proceeding."

What happens is that the very things you do to solve the problem become the problem. When you continue to do what is not working, you make it worse. The more you see your wife withdrawing, the more you may try to do. The more you pursue her, the more she withdraws. If she had any doubts when she began the process of leaving, your pursuit, instead of allowing her to get in touch with her feelings about ending the marriage, is usually counterproductive. She ignores your efforts because all she may be able to focus on is her contempt for you. If you want to save the marriage, you have to use a different approach or you will push her out the door. Stop pursuing. Stop the flowers, stop the love notes. Try a 180-degree turn.

Don't pursue her for status checks on your relationship. Men tend always to want to know where the relationship is. The talk about the future and marriage has to stop. All your wife will talk about are her feelings about the past. Give her the opportunity to collect neutral or positive experiences so next time you talk she may have something positive to say. Let her feel that you are moving forward with your life. This is the opposite of what most guys actually do, observes Weiner-Davis. Give your wife the opportunity to get in touch with what her life will be like after you. If you come off desperate and clingy, you won't seem attractive. Get a life and show her you will be okay no matter what, and she may become more interested. It takes time, but it works. "Sometimes miracles happen. Sometimes it's too late, but even if you can't save the marriage, these tactics will still help you restore your self-esteem." This will help you get your feet back on the ground no matter how things end up.

For more information, try Weiner-Davis's Web site: www.divorcebusters.com.

1

Before You File for Divorce: What You Need to Know

Rule #1. Be Decisive about the State of Your Marriage

If you're not happy with your marriage, then do something about your situation. But don't cheat. Either work on your marriage or get out. Don't tell the women at the bar you're unhappy, tell your wife. Be honest with yourself and with her. Whatever the problem is—whether you're not proud of her, or you don't like your sex life, tell her and give her a chance to change. Remember, it's cheaper to keep her! If you can fall in love and out of love, you can fall back in love again.

If you leave her for someone else, you're more likely to have an angry divorce. Men rarely leave a marriage unless another woman is waiting. Men just don't take this important advice, notes Lynne Gold-Bikin of Wolf, Block, Schorr & Solis-Cohen, in Norristown, Pennsylvania. This is why, she notes, the divorce process becomes so angry and costly. The ex-wife who has been betrayed will be bitter.

Rule #2. Don't Be Confrontational

"Compromise is better than confrontation," says Barry Croland, Esq., Shapiro & Croland, Hackensack, New Jersey. You're better off trying to build bridges, not battles. Whereas marriage may be about trust, divorce is not. Don't exacerbate the problems with vengeful or half-true statements, or baseless claims. "Take the high road, let your lawyers fight your battles," suggests Amy J. Amundsen. The acrimonious nature of divorce is a societal phenomenon that focuses on the negative and on the need to "win." This attitude doesn't help anyone. Instead, try to be honest about your own imperfections and take responsibility for the failure of your marriage. Consider reading a book about how to communicate and negotiate affirmatively and fairly. In most divorces, compromise is not what occurs; instead, a great amount of anger has to be diffused.

Rule #3. Don't Let the Divorce Process Become a War Zone

Recognize that in this process the deeper you get, the more you both lose. It's tempting, especially with a hard-nosed lawyer, to hold your ground, but you have to find a line that allows damage control. Try not to escalate your losses in an avoidable acrimonious situation, especially when it comes to your children. If things get hot, focus on what is in the best interests of the kids, not on the animosity. Ask yourself what's best for you in the long run, in particular for your relationship with your kids.

There's really not much you can do when your wife's lawyer is stoking the emotional fires. Lawyers will often feed into a wife who says "up the ante," "pursue him." You may not be able to do much to affect your wife or her lawyer, but you can still control your response, advises Stanley Teitelbaum, a psychotherapist in Teaneck, New Jersey. If your ex makes blatantly untrue accusations, don't take the bait. Don't play the game. Consider mediation, which can be less adversarial.

Rule #4. Keep Your Cool

"It's only a game, it's only a game, it's only a game."

Okay, divorce is not really a game, but you need to keep some perspective if the divorce gets ugly. Your wife's attorney may coach her in ways to bait you by seeking out and focusing on your hot buttons. Their goal is to make you explode and engage in conduct that can be used against you in court. So close your eyes, calm down, recite your mantra, grit your teeth, and go on. Don't fall prey to intentional antagonism or baiting.

Take up Ti Chi, meditation, or whatever works for you, but ice down those hot buttons.

Control your temper; violence will only hurt you. Any violent act you commit against your ex-wife, no matter the circumstances, will work particularly against sharing time with your children and will dramatically harm you in any negotiations or court trial. No matter what the temptation or motives, control yourself. Never threaten your wife in any manner. A comment like, "If you leave you'll be a pauper," is inappropriate.

Write down a list of goals and read it each morning (more often if necessary). Committing goals to writing always makes them more attainable. Review the list frequently to embed it in your mind. Your list can include:

- ✔ I won't lose my temper no matter what my ex does.

- ✔ I will keep my eye on the long term: my new life and my children.

- ✔ I can't control the process, but I can control my reactions to it.

5

Rule #5. Don't Do Anything Illegal

"Your ex may have a voice-activated tape recorder she will use to get information on tape to use in custody or other situations," warns Barry Croland, Esq., a matrimonial attorney in Hackensack, New Jersey. And you might think it would help to have a tape recording of your wife saying: "You'll never see the kids unless you give me the money I want!" or "You can bet I'll tell the kids about you and your mistress." Although you might think that this would help convey a truer picture of her to a court, your tapes may differ greatly from what she says at a deposition or in court under oath. "There are big risks with this game because the judge may be turned off and it will be counterproductive," cautions Croland.

Before you even think about taping, consult your lawyer about the legalities and risks. Even if your lawyer says it's okay legally (which it may not be), consider what this will do to the divorce process. You're seriously upping the ante. If you're caught, your wife will know you're the sneaky, conniving, slime she thought you were. And she's probably right. Secretively taping someone is not the best way to build bridges toward a settlement.

Rule #6. Get the Skeletons out of Your Closet

If you have skeletons in your closet—whether financial or with blonde hair and blue eyes—discuss these up front with your attorney.

Bombs exploding late in the game will be harder to contain. You are always better off planning up front with your lawyer how to deal with these issues. You may be able to avoid an ugly situation or at least control the damage. You don't want your indiscretion coming out for the first time on a nasty cross-exam by your wife's attorney after you've been on the witness stand for a long day. If you have children, spare them the additional anguish of having skeletons come out without warning.

Rule #7. Don't Push Your Wife's Hot Buttons

It's tempting. If you can make your ex-wife flip out, you'll get momentary pleasure, but in the end you'll get misery back. "Think in full circles," advises Michele Weiner-Davis. Don't be short-sighted for immediate gratification. "What goes around comes around." Your attorney's advice to take an action that you know will hurt, insult, or egg on your ex may be right from a strategic legal perspective, but for your mental health, you may have to stop fighting. You can win the battle by pushing a hot button (or lots of them), but you'll lose the war.

Rule #8. Clean Up Your Life

This means more than taking a regular shower. If you have an alcohol problem, prescription drug habit, or any substance abuse problem, clean up your act as quickly as possible. These matters will seriously jeopardize any custody negotiations or other aspects of the divorce. If you need professional help, get it. For example, if you undertake counseling and your wife doesn't, this fact could weigh positively in your favor at trial. If you need to take any steps to show your life in a more positive light, your lawyer may be able to guide you in doing so.

Assume that your wife is recording in great detail (she probably is!) every stupid and inappropriate act that you commit. So clean up your behavior. "Act as if a private investigator is following you," cautions Amy J. Amundsen.

Rule #9. Become a Model Citizen If You Aren't Already

Join a church, synagogue, mosque, or other religious organization, whatever is appropriate. Become active in your community and in worthwhile charity organizations; volunteer some time. Make a donation to several charities (even if they are modest in amount) to show your commitment to a good cause.

Carve out some time to spend with your children and document it. You can save stubs from basketball games, movie theaters, and other items in your photo album.

Be a good Joe and find objective ways to demonstrate it. The real benefit of all of these steps is that you really should be a good Joe anyhow. Giving to the community, becoming active or involved in spiritual matters, and spending quality time with your kids are really what life is all about.

Rule #10. Limit Future Involvement with Your Wife

To the extent feasible, try to negotiate as many arrangements as possible that give you a clean break with your wife. Opt for property settlements versus alimony to the extent you can. Negotiate detailed visitation and other specific rights and obligations to avoid future negotiations. Whatever you can do to minimize future involvements, especially financial, the better for you and your ex-wife.

Rule #11. Don't Assume Your Prenuptial Agreement Is Carved in Stone

If you have a prenuptial agreement, be certain that all the appropriate exhibits and financial disclosures are attached. If you didn't make adequate financial disclosures, or if your wife wasn't represented by her own lawyer, she will have a good chance of overturning it. If there are any questions about validity, changed circumstances, or other issues, address them up front as quickly as possible with your attorney. Get your records together to show that you made full disclosure when you signed the agreement and that your wife was represented by counsel, and collect any other items that will help uphold a prenuptial agreement.

Prenuptial agreements require care, especially in a community property state like California, observes Ginita Wall, an accountant in San Diego. "I had a client who kept his separate property in a trust in his name alone. He never deposited any community monies to the account, or so he thought. As it turns out, he had periodically loaned money from his trust account to the family to buy a house, take trips, and so on. When the community property had surplus cash, he repaid the money to the separate property trust. Even though he thought these transfers were simply loan repayments, the court characterized them as community property. He had to analyze years of statements and treat each repayment, and the earnings attributable to it, as community property."

Rule #12. Keep a Low Profile

If you are doing something stupid and inappropriate, at least have enough sense not to advertise. In too many cases, soon-to-be-ex-husbands have left a brazen trail of American Express receipts that have enabled investigators to construct a detailed schedule of their infidelity—from the restaurants, plays, and hotel rooms, to the purchases of negligees and perfume. If you are doing something that you shouldn't be doing, at least pay cash. If you want to advertise it, there are newspapers that will make it more obvious than the American Express receipts will at your trial.

Sound obvious and silly? You would be amazed at the stupid things people do. One husband moved to Arizona and argued that his business obligations prevented him from flying to New York for a deposition. When his business was appraised, the appraiser copied American Express receipts that his wife's lawyer used to reconstruct an itinerary listing hotels he stayed at, restaurants he ate at, and plays he attended while on little jaunts to New York City. The only thing the receipts didn't disclose was the name of his mistress. Don't be careless with the little things, they can be really telling.

"One husband had been having an affair for eight years before his ex found out about it," notes Ginita Wall, a San Diego forensic accountant. "The husband lavished his paramour with gifts and presents, jewelry, flowers, and other not-so-inexpensive trinkets. The wife tried to argue that the jewelry was marital property on which she should have a claim. To identify the information to proceed I contacted the various jewelers in the area. We eventually uncovered twice as many jewelry purchases as the wife had guessed!" The husband might have thought he was being careful, but the trail of credit card receipts, store records, and personal checks exposed him and his infidelity.

One of the most ridiculous situations involved a husband who kept photographs of him and his girlfriend in indiscreet poses in his night-table drawer. His wife innocently stumbled on them one afternoon while searching for their passports. Don't let your arrogance cause you to think you're not accountable, because you are.

Rule #13. Negotiate from the Positive: Concentrate on What You Agree on First

Begin with points you both agree on, even if they seem small. As you work out an arrangement, commit it to writing. It's a lot easier to sign off on one or two matters at a time than an entire divorce settlement because it allows you to build on agreements instead of focusing on disagreements.

Rule #14. Don't Threaten Your Ex-Wife

Violence or even threats of violence will cost you. All you have to do is make a "terroristic threat," and in some states, this alone is enough to get you thrown out of the house. This could be something as hyperbolic as "When you're sleeping tonight honey, I'm going to carve out your heart." But if your wife believes she is in jeopardy or if she is put into a state of alarm, or if she can convince a judge of either, you could be sleeping on the street. So zip your lip.

If you harass your wife, follow or stalk her, or make her feel she is in danger, that may also be enough, even without words, to get you thrown out of your house. You can be removed permanently! If you then violate the restraining order the court placed on you, you can be incarcerated. This is serious stuff. Some wives will try to bait their ex. False allegations have been made many times. Consider having a witness move into the house with you. It may help to divide the house up, as in the movie *War of the Roses,* to give each of you your own space. In some instances, if you are able, it may be best just to move out, suggests Lynne Strober, Esq., of Mandelbaum, Salsburg, Gold, Lazris, Discenza & Steinberg, in West Orange, New Jersey. However, such an approach creates two households which have to be supported. Photograph or videotape everything before moving.

Rule #15. Keep in Mind That Men and Women Approach Divorce Differently

Understanding these differences can help you get a better result, avoid setting your wife off, and limit the antagonism, notes Stanley

Teitelbaum, a family counselor in Teaneck, New Jersey. Disentangle the financial side from the emotional side, he suggests. "Money is power and many men start to use money as their wedge to make their statement and they get lost in this. It becomes a whole power play." You must focus on what needs to be done to disentangle you and your ex so you can go forward. If you controlled your family checkbook and finances, you must turn over control of her financial life to your ex-wife. You can't continue to use money to control her. Divorce is often a charged negotiation process, and it's helpful for you to realize that you may be prone to operate in an emotional way; instead, operating from a perspective of somewhat detached rationality will help you get through this.

Rule #16. Know Your Stuff: What Does Your Wife Really Want?

The key to everything in your divorce is knowledge of the facts: finance, assets, liabilities, needs of your wife, concerns of the children, what the legal process entails. The importance to your wife of each element is essential if you want to minimize the trauma of the divorce process. Being a good listener is a vital quality to obtain the knowledge you need. You must also make a concerted effort to get informed. Organize your legal (wills, deed, etc.), tax (old returns, audit notes, etc.), and financial (brokerage statements, investment materials, etc.) data. Understand what you have. Read, listen, ask, collect information. Divorce books, seminars, and help from your advisors can educate you.

Rule #17. Know What Your Household Expenses Really Add Up To

You may have tended to business and career matters and have no familiarity with household expenditures. Nevertheless, you must now acquaint yourself with the cost of running your home to participate intelligently in the child support and alimony determinations. If you don't and there is a disagreement over the stipulated amount, your wife may say: "I take care of the books and financial records and my husband doesn't know anything about it . . ." And your ignorance will make your position tenuous.

To be fair, you must understand what the family is spending for maintenance of the house, automobile expenses, clothing, and so on. The resolution should be predicated on facts, not supposition.

Rule #18. Be Familiar with Your Children's Lives

You should know your children's teachers, doctors, friends, school schedules, and after-school activities. It's never too late to involve yourself in quality time with your children. You can spend time with your child going to a sporting event after school or watch your child participate in some event. It's easy for a parent who works to consult a school schedule to find out what is going on.

If you are seeking custody, you need to be an active parent. Do you know who are your child's best friends? When does your child go to the dentist? How much time do you spend with the child? What position does the child play in Little League? You don't have to be involved in every aspect of your child's life, but being a substantial part of your child's life is what being a dad is about. Getting a lawyer who acts like a hired gun to pursue custody may work, but does it? What you should really want is a quality relationship with your children. To do this, you need to understand them and their lives. Know what is important to them. Earn custody, if you can, with caring and interest in your children, not through a legal battle.

When you get divorced, there is a redefinition of the previous relationships with your now ex-wife and your children. If you love the children and understand that there will be a redefinition, you have to involve yourself more in their lives and reassure them that they have no responsibility for what occurred and that both parents will be there for them.

Rule #19. Know Your Wife's Spending Habits and Budgets for Childcare Expenses

Men are often so busy working they leave all the paperwork to their wives. These men have no idea what assets there are, no clue as to expenses; some don't even know their own bank account numbers! You must be cognizant of these matters. During your divorce, you have to detail the expenses of the marriage. If you don't know what is being spent on groceries, clothing for the kids, and so on, find out. Many men cannot even guess what it costs to clothe a child because the mother has bought the kids' wardrobe. If you make a claim for expansive visitation, say 50–50, or even full custody, you have to be knowledgeable about the children's expenses. "You can't simply say that whatever the mother puts down on an expense statement is 'too much,' that doesn't show any knowledge," notes

Jonathan Pollack, a New York matrimonial attorney with Beldock, Levine & Hoffman, in New York City.

If you want to control child support payments and alimony payments and make the best case for child visitation or custody, get details on the direct expenses of the marriage, especially those of the child. If you've been making regular payments for specific direct expenses of your child, it is more likely that a court will permit this type of continued payment, rather than require you to make periodic lump sum payments that your ex, and not you, will control. "Alternatively, a father can't knowingly dispute what the mother claims the needs of the child are, if he can't present a legitimate argument of something different," says Pollack. The moral is if you don't have the details, your ex will have more control and money. Before you move out of the home, start going shopping with the kids on your own and involve yourself on an equal basis. Be aware of what the mother spends on the children. Did your wife spend within a budget when the family was intact? If she did, and you can prove it, you'll have a much better shot at controlling what she can spend after.*

If you're not keeping the check register, try to. Examine canceled checks each month and keep a tally of basic expenses for the household, living costs, the children, and your wife.

If your wife has done all the shopping, begin to look at what things cost. "Wives frequently change spending patterns when they begin to suspect a divorce," says Pollack. The wives are told they are going to have to justify their expenses since this may affect their right to alimony or child support. The wives will be told that whatever they spend, they will get from the courts—so, many

---

*For additional information on budgets, organizing finances, and templates to use, see: Shenkman *The Beneficiary Workbook* (John Wiley & Sons, 1999).

wives spend more!" This increased spending could obviously affect your finances adversely.

"Another problem," notes Pollack, "men feel guilty when they're the ones leaving. So what do they do? They buy more for their wives. The result is that this could support a higher alimony or child support payment later!" Meanwhile, because of anger over the deteriorating marital situation, the wife may take her frustration out on their credit cards. The situation can spiral out of control. Pollack sometimes sees this spending frenzy last as long as six months. "When you later try to reduce expenditures to something you can afford, it gets tough."

"If you think your paycheck is disappearing as fast as you deposit it, carefully evaluate expenses," cautions Pollack. "Try to get your wife, if she is dependent on your income, to budget." There is also a fine line between your being too lax, and being too miserly. "If you get too cheap, you may just push your wife to move for support even sooner," cautions Pollack. The ideal approach is to agree who will pay for what bills.

Rule #20. Know Your Wife's Financial Dealings

Be certain that you have knowledge, detail, and corroboration of your wife's independent income or separate assets, as this will be critical in the divorce process. Document your wife's expenses. (Does she rival Imelda Marcos with her shoe collection?) Any dissipation of marital assets can be vital to demonstrate. Unusual or wasteful spending, intentional damage to the marital home, or other waste may be helpful ammunition when negotiating maintenance or property settlements.

Rule #21. Know What Your Wife's Assets Are

Try to get a handle on your wife's independent assets: IRA accounts, pensions (there are often more than one account), inheritances, jewelry (especially gifts received that you may not be aware of). The sooner you collect information, the better. The closer to the divorce you wait, the more difficult it will be to obtain facts.

"Use some common sense when obtaining information," warns Pollack. "Don't get caught rifling through your wife's pocketbook. One husband was caught red-handed using a flashlight to search his wife's pocketbook late at night. The wife caught him looking through personal notes. This conduct underscored for the court the wife's claims that the home environment was so bad that the wife should be permitted to leave with the daughter."

When you're doing your homework, you're allowed to look at bank statements, canceled checks, and other marital financial documents, not your wife's private papers. For example, a canceled check to a bank you're not aware of could be a payment for a safe deposit box where jewelry or account books are stashed. Although you're entitled to get marital financial information through the discovery process, having it in advance can be helpful. If you can discreetly copy documents, these can serve as a test to see if you're getting all the information later. Also, this information can be useful to disprove later claims of the wife regarding her financial needs.

"Be alert for foreign accounts, cash in a safe deposit box, and other items which may be difficult to prove later," suggests Pollack. "Another trick is for your wife to prepay amounts to stores and services she uses regularly," notes Amy J. Amundsen.

Rule #22. Understand the Legal Process of Divorce

Understanding the judicial process will help you keep the lawyers and the process under control. Make sure to hire a lawyer who can explain both strengths and weaknesses of your case as well as your alternatives: mediation, arbitration, even therapeutic resolutions to solve issues relevant to your children. The best solution for custody cases and visitation can be a trained therapist. The court is not the best place if there is physical or sexual abuse, or a total denial of access to the children. It should be the last place someone goes as it relates to the children. The therapist will mediate and assist in establishing visitation. This practice is becoming more common because family court is often bogged down with so many custody cases.

Finding the right attorney for you is covered in Chapter 2.

2

Finding the Right Lawyer

Rule #23. Consider <u>Not</u> Hiring a Lawyer, to Save Money

If you and your wife are on relatively good terms, if there are no children involved, and if your assets are modest in size and relatively straightforward to divide, you might want to sit down and distribute the assets so that each feels the outcome is fair and equitable. Hypothetically, she might get the house and maintenance and other support, if needed, and you might keep your IRA, annual bonus, and the summer cottage. Once you have agreed mutually to these and other terms, you and your wife can continue to save legal fees by doing the court filing yourself if it's practical in your state. The actual filing costs may be as little as $500. In some states, the process can be much like registering your new car as opposed to having the dealer do it. Numerous divorce kits are available to help you with this paperwork.

A smarter alternative would be for you and your spouse to at least pay an attorney to review your proposed settlement and court documents. A consultation with a matrimonial specialist is worth the cost to obtain the peace of mind that you haven't overlooked a major issue. Also, if you each have a lawyer review the document, representation by independent counsel, will make it harder for your ex to challenge the agreement in the future.

When considering going it alone, don't forget the old adage, "don't be penny wise and pound foolish." One Casanova married and divorced three times. Each time, out of guilt (he always had a younger beauty in the wings), he signed divorce agreements presented to him by his soon-to-be-ex's attorney. He never had the sense to hire his own lawyer: As a doctor, he didn't have much love for lawyers and just didn't want to hire one. His reward? After a lifetime of work, tremendous earnings, and establishment of an international reputation as a leader in his field, with all his payments to his three ex-wives, he barely makes ends meet. He'll never be able to save enough for retirement.

The moral is that it always makes sense to work intelligently with your lawyers to minimize costs. Watch the clock and don't shoot the breeze. Be prepared with copies of all documents and other relevant information. But inadequate legal help can prove to be far more costly. This is especially true as your income, net worth, and the complexity of your case increase.

Rule #24. Pick the Right Lawyer for Your Case

Do not hire an attorney simply because your accountant, golf buddy, or a friend has recommended him or her. Word of mouth recommendations are helpful, but keep in mind that you need someone who is a matrimonial specialist.

Knowledge is everything. You need an attorney who is knowledgeable of the law, of the issues that affect finance, assets, liabilities, needs of the other side, children, and so forth. The attorney must be skilled enough to be sensitive to the other side of your case (your wife's viewpoint). Being a good listener is vital. Understanding the judicial process is critical if your case may go to trial.

But matrimonial expertise is not enough. "A good attorney, if they pick up any reticence by either you or your wife, they will encourage mediation or therapy . . . this is a great sign for an attorney," recommends Michele Weiner-Davis author of *Divorce Busting*.

Rule #24. Pick the Right Lawyer for Your Case

Tell the attorney you want to be reasonable. Some attorneys want to establish fair and appropriate settlements. Listen to cues in the initial interview. Is the attorney talking about pressure and destruction, or inundating your wife with legal documents and procedures? Is that really going to get you and your family the result you want? Listen to how the attorney talks about your spouse. If the attorney sounds as if he or she just wants to start a war, if the attorney seems too adversarial, don't go forward. Hire a different attorney.

You don't want someone who encourages you to fight. You want an attitude of solving a problem. This cuts down on cost and leaves you more in control. You cannot guarantee you are going to get a judge who fully understands the nuances of your case. Even if you are fortunate enough to get such a judge, it doesn't mean his or her decision will be favorable to you. If you negotiate for a settlement, you have more control and minimize the risks and tremendous expenses of going to court. Your ex is still the person you married, you don't have to make it a war or even exchange nasty comments. You want an attorney who is sensitive to this approach, recommends Lynne Strober, Esq., of Mandelbaum, Salsburg, Gold, Lazris, Discenza & Steinberg of West Orange, New Jersey.

The lawyer must be a problem solver and not a fighter. Most clients ask matrimonial lawyers, "Are you tough?" The real question should be, "Are you effective?" The same approach applies to fees. You may not want to pay $350 per hour, but paying $150 per hour may not be better. You must be sensitive to costs, but the question is: "Who can accomplish a fair resolution in the shortest period of time, for the least amount of money, and with the most lasting result," says Barry Croland, Esq., Shapiro & Croland, Hackensack, New Jersey. So don't be cheap: it could cost you more in the long run.

Rule #25. Interview Your Attorney Thoroughly before You Hire

When you interview a prospective attorney, consider asking the following questions:

- How long have you practiced in the field of matrimonial law?

- What proportion of your practice is confined to matrimonial and family law matters?

- Do you want to "go for the jugular" or do you prefer to mediate and settle amicably? (The former approach never works in the long run, so forget it!)

- What other areas of practice and experience do you have?

- What size of divorce case to you typically handle in terms of assets and income?

- Do you handle any other particular specialty areas within divorce? This could relate to closely held businesses, pension matters, artists, and so forth. Artists, sports figures, and so forth have unique legal and financial issues, so hiring a matrimonial attorney whose firm also has this experience can be helpful.

- Does your office have adequate staffing to assist me in my case? How many associates do you have? How many paralegals do you employ? What level of personnel would generally be helping me? (Don't assume that simply because a paralegal or secretaries will be helping with your case that this is inappropriate. There is no reason to incur attorney fees when a paraprofessional can handle certain routine matters. You just want to be sure that the attorney will be available if and when he or she is needed.)

✔ How do you bill? What ancillary charges might arise? How will your payments be secured? Do you want a mortgage on my house to make sure fees are paid?

✔ Are your bills sufficiently detailed to determine exactly what was done? (Never accept a bill that says "for services rendered," or even a bulk paragraph listing several lines of text and then a number. Insist on a bill that lists at minimum time charges separately for each attorney; each day, or acts done, and the specific charges for it.)

Finally, if you know your wife's attorney, ask the lawyer you are interviewing whether he or she has had any dealings with that attorney and whether there would be any problem working opposite that attorney.

Rule #26. Get Your Information Together to Reduce Your Legal Fees

Any lawyer who properly represents you (and any lawyer who properly represents your spouse), will need detailed disclosure of information. Too often, one or the other of the spouses fights and delays giving the necessary information. Although withholding information has undoubtedly benefited some husbands (because their ex's attorneys gave up pursuing getting the real information) in most cases all it does is increase both lawyers' bills because they have to pursue the information they reasonably need and are entitled to. There's no question that some wives' lawyers have abused the system by seeking information they don't really need just to harass a husband and/or to run up bills, but this is the exception. If you can put together and provide the information both lawyers will need up front, you can save time and reduce your legal costs. And if you make some effort to organize the data, you can further improve the time and cost savings.

What documents and information are needed? Start with the following and ask your lawyer if he or she needs anything else:

Three years' prior tax returns. Arrange these in a looseleaf binder with a tab for each year and a tab separating out the state tax returns (e.g., "1999 Federal," "1999 State"). Be certain to attach all schedules. If ancillary information is necessary to understand the return, attach it as well behind another tab, "1999 Ancillary Info." For example, if you have a home-based business, you report your income and deductions on Form 1040, Schedule C. If you have a business car or any equipment, you will report depreciation there. The tax form itself will not reflect the details concerning each item of equipment, what you paid for it, when it was purchased, and so forth. You should have a supplemental schedule listing this information and the depreciation claimed. Attach a copy as an ancillary form because your attorney (and your wife's) will need this and so will the accountant who helps value your business.

Business documents. If you have a separate business, organize copies of key business documents in a loose-leaf binder with tabs. Include copies of the legal documents used to form the entity (e.g., a certificate of incorporation), three years' prior tax returns, a balance sheet if the tax return doesn't include one, copies of key contracts and agreements (e.g., partnership agreement, lease for your office), payroll information, and anything else that might be pertinent. You will have to have the business valued, but this probably should be coordinated with the attorneys representing both you and your wife.

Copy of your wills and any other estate-planning documents (e.g., powers of attorney, living wills, insurance trusts).

A comprehensive personal balance sheet. List each asset, its approximate value, account numbers if applicable, the manner in which it is owned (e.g., you alone, your wife alone, joint), and any pertinent comments to help the attorneys understand what is involved.

For any assets other than cash and stock, attach valuation data.

If you own a house, have a real estate broker give you a comparative market analysis. Attach a copy of the deed.

Provide a copy of retirement plans and a recent statement.

Include home mortgage and equity line applications.

Copy your mortgage.

Copy the key pages of every insurance policy: life, disability, homeowners, and so on.

Copy all car registrations and the blue book value.

List your home assets.

List jewelry and art. Take pictures of any expensive items. Really valuable items will often have to be appraised.

The best way to present the balance sheet data is to put together a loose-leaf binder. Indicate the balance sheet data first, by preparing either a computer report or a handwritten schedule. Set up tabs behind the balance sheet, using the same order shown there, for each item that has additional detailed information.

Providing this comprehensive information can build tremendous goodwill since it will demonstrate your desire to be fair and to disclose (rather than hide) key information. If the process seems time consuming and a hassle, it is. And that's the whole point. It's always more economical for *you* to spend hours organizing your own information than to pay attorneys to organize it for you. And because it's your information, you'll do a much quicker job of organizing it.

Rule #27. Make Sure You Control the Divorce Process

It's your life, not the lawyer's. You must take control of your lawyer and your case and encourage your wife to do the same. You can do this while still working effectively with your attorney. Ask your attorney to make settlement offers. This may force your wife's attorney to respond and thereby narrow the issues.

A lot of the craziness that occurs in the divorce process is caused by matrimonial lawyers who get so wrapped up in issues that they take things personally and begin playing games. Matrimonial mediation can be an effective alternative. Many people get divorced without animosity; they simply want closure, and they don't want to spend a fortune on the divorce. If that describes your situation, then hire a mediator to work out the terms, and then just have lawyers finalize the agreement, without bloodshed.

Rule #27. Make Sure You Control the Divorce Process

The matrimonial bar, of course, doesn't want this process to happen: It's bad for business. So what can you do if your wife takes the opposite approach and hires an attorney who goes for blood? Nothing: "It's absolutely terrible," observes Colleen A. Brown, Esq., partner in Lawrence, Werner, Kesselring, Swartout & Brown, LLP, Canandaigua, New York. That type of attitude will assure higher fees and more animosity. Perhaps the only thing you can do is resist the temptation to lower yourself to the same level.

Most of the cases that incur the cost and difficulties of court litigation start out with a high level of hostility. To diffuse that level, you must hire a lawyer who will not isolate you from the process but will keep you informed. You should have meetings with your attorney to hear what is going on. And if matters are not proceeding constructively toward a reasonable conclusion, you must intercede, recommends Barry Croland, Esq., of Hackensack, New Jersey. Again, your future, your wife's future, and your children's future are at stake.

The divorce process is based on an adversarial system, much like a criminal trial. "Your case shouldn't be handled as if it were 'Husband Smith v. Wife Smith,' it should be handled with the attitude that the case is the 'Smith Family Case,'" advises David L. Levy, Esq., cofounder and president of the Children's Rights Council based in Washington, D.C.

Because the divorce process is adversarial, you should never give up your rights to full participation. It is too easy to accept control by the system. Listen to your lawyer's cues, but remember, it's your case that he's driving. "Wiggle-room" always tends to be present in the law. The cases which make up much of the "divorce law" are based on the specific facts the court looked at. Every divorce, including yours, has its own unique circumstances. So there is always some room for interpretation as to how to apply the law to your case. You must take control of it as well as the negotiation of strategies. Remain boss of the wiggle-room.

Rule #28. Make Sure Meetings with Your Ex and the Lawyers Are Productive

There are lawyers who won't have meetings with you and your wife. They may not understand problem solving or may fear bringing two angry people together. But diffusion of anger early in the divorce process is usually good. It's better for the anger to come out in a meeting than to fester, worsen, and flood out years later in a court proceeding.

Some lawyers also prefer to polarize the parties. If this starts, ask the lawyer to have a meeting. If the attorney says no, ask why? If the lawyer cannot arrange meetings together, maybe you should find another lawyer.

If your ex-wife is combative, don't play "King of the Mountain" or try to prove you're tougher. Keep your cool. Say, "I'm sorry you feel that way, but I want to solve the problem. Can you tell me why you don't think my approach is fair?"

Don't take over a meeting to prove how smart you are. Meetings must focus on problem solving. You don't solve problems by fighting. If your ex or her attorney makes a wildly unreasonable demand, instead of countering with an equally absurd proposal, ask reasonable questions. If, for example, they ask for $100,000 a year in alimony and your net income after taxes is only modestly above that amount—ask "How can we do that?" "Where do you think the money will come from?" Reasonable questions may bring the discussion back to reality. "In most divorce cases, the people have limited abilities to communicate. The lawyer should try to be a shepherd to help you and your ex communicate," advises Barry Croland, Esq., Hackensack, New Jersey.

Rule #29. Make Sure Your Wife Has Proper Legal and Financial Representation

Sound like the opposite of what you really want? Wrong! If your wife does not have representation by competent counsel and input from knowledgeable financial professionals (e.g., an accountant to apprize her and her lawyer of tax and financial considerations), the chances are far greater that she will later repetition the court to modify the divorce settlement. Competent representation is usually much better, even if her attorneys aggressively represent your ex, because less experienced advisers may pursue unreasonable demands or inappropriate investigations. A well-respected professional has a reputation to lose. You want the best professionals you can get on both sides, yours and your ex's. Competent matrimonial experts will be far less likely to make major issues out of small points and will be more likely to seek a reasonable settlement. If your business assets are complex, the more capable your wife's attorney the more quickly you may be able to reach a reasonable solution. Contrast this with your wife have a less skilled attorney who, because he doesn't understand the issues, is afraid to settle quickly for fear of making a mistake.

Rule #30. Consider Arbitration as an Option

Arbitration is yet another approach to the divorce process. In arbitration, an outside party (called an arbitrator) makes the ultimate decision in your case, and it cannot be appealed. You come to the meeting with your attorney and present your case, as does your spouse.

Why would you want to go to arbitration rather than face the court? First, timing: it could take months to get on a judge's calendar. Second, you may have no financial resources left due to the cost of pretrial hearings (e.g., for your separation agreement). Third, emotionally, you may not want to go through with any more hearings and paperwork. And fourth, arbitration may be less expensive than the trial process depending on the state you live in. Even if not less expensive it can still be quicker and less adversarial. Carefully discuss the pros and cons of this approach with your attorney before committing to it and especially discuss why your attorney believes arbitration is appropriate in your particular case.

Rule #31. Consider Mediation as an Option

Unlike arbitration, mediation is not binding. Mediation uses a neutral third party to help you resolve issues without the cost, delays, and adversarial atmosphere that the legal system can foster. "Mediation is the way to go if you can," says Michele Weiner-Davis.

Mediation works only when two mature people can sit down and discuss their differences without rancor or hostility. It is much less expensive than hiring divorce attorneys. This system is most successful when you both are completely honest about your income, insurance policies, debts, and savings accounts—in essence, all your tangible assets.

Be willing to enter mediation over major points you feel you must secure. Even lawyers get too heated up and become unconsciously blinded. When the process gets stuck, third-party mediators are very useful, especially nonlawyers, who can keep the process at the layperson level. But try to set up binding rather than nonbinding mediation sessions. Lawyers for both sides still will be involved, but function as sideliners until agreements have been reached. This is how mediation can save costs. The mediator, not two opposing lawyers, structures the settlement. Then the lawyers work out the details and commit it to writing.

In some situations, mediation can be better than the time and expense of a trial. If you and your spouse can control your feelings and address the divorce rationally, mediation can be a wise option. If you prefer mediation, remember that in general, it only works when you and your wife are on relatively equal footing. If you're substantially more financially astute, mediating financial issues may be unfair to your wife. If you're not equal in knowledge or experience, using experts can help. For example, an accountant to explain budget issues. Or, the matrimonial attorneys might handle certain key financial issues and then send specific issues for you and your spouse to address with a mediator, suggests Lynne Strober, Esq., of Mandelbaum, Salsburg, Gold, Lazris, Discenza & Steinberg, West Orange, New Jersey.

Another option is to mediate one or two points, even if attorneys are negotiating the rest of your matters. For example, you could use a family therapist or child psychologist to mediate visitation issues and a matrimonial mediator with financial expertise to mediate business and financial issues.

When all the issues are settled, the mediator will prepare a document that an attorney can review. At this point, both you and your spouse will each want to hire an attorney to examine the agreement. One of them will then prepare the other paperwork for submission for the divorce.

Rule #32. Find a Qualified Mediator

"Mediation is only as good as the mediator. You have to carefully investigate the background of the person who is mediating," cautions Barry Croland, Esq., Shapiro & Croland, Hackensack, New Jersey.

How do you find a qualified mediator? Networking is an ideal way. First explain the situation to your family physician. He or she will give you the names of inidividual psychologists, social workers, and family counselors who handle divorce mediation cases. Once you find someone, ask the following questions:

- ✔ How long have you practiced?

- ✔ How many mediations have you been involved in?

- ✔ Do you work closely with lawyers on your cases? If the answer is yes, please give me a specific example.

- ✔ How much do you charge?

- ✔ Ask for references.

Rule #33. Don't Use the Court System for Revenge

There are lots of ways in the world to get revenge, but don't try doing it through the legal process. Not only is revenge generally ineffective, but it is extraordinarily costly and will create far more trauma and difficulty for everyone involved including yourself, and especially your children if you have any. If you need to vent your anger, save yourself a bundle and buy a punching bag instead.

Rule #34. When Your Divorce Is Finalized, Get Your File

When your case is eventually settled, ask your lawyer to return your file. You should retain copies of all documents and retrieve all personal financial and other data. Set up a file with the final agreements, court papers, expert reports, and so forth. This will be helpful for planning to get back on your feet financially, updating your will, and if your ex challenges something in the future.

Nonessential documents might best be shredded. In one case, a well-known attorney filed for bankruptcy after his divorce. The IRS came into possession of a host of files from his divorce (which he hadn't shredded) and other items, all to his utter dismay. Nevertheless, ask your attorney before you destroy any documents.

Rule #35. Update Your Estate Planning Documents to Keep Your Wife from Getting All Your Assets

Even though state law may provide that following a divorce your wife won't have rights or powers under your will or other documents (except to the extent agreed to in the divorce settlement), don't wait for the divorce to be finalized to address these issues. Do it now!

Make sure your wife does not have access to your bank accounts. You've heard many stories about soon-to-be ex-wives emptying out joint bank accounts before the split. You may have also given your wife the opportunity to empty your own accounts as well!

Married couples commonly name each other agent under a power of attorney as part of any estate plan. In most of these powers of attorney, you may have granted your wife immediate authority to act (i.e., without first having to demonstrate that you are disabled) in a broad range of legal, tax, and financial matters. If a divorce is imminent, your wife may use or abuse the power of attorney to empty out bank, brokerage, or other accounts.

You should therefore take two steps immediately, under the direction of your attorney. First, revoke her power of attorney. This may require sending her a specific form revoking the power of attorney (the rules differ from state to state and may depend on the language in the power of attorney you signed naming her agent). Ask your attorney whether the document revoking the power can be filed to make it a public record. Second, have a new power of attorney prepared naming someone else as agent. This is vital to protect yourself in the event you become ill or disabled.

Rule #36. Make Sure Your Wife No Longer Has Authority to Tell the Doctors to "Pull the Plug" on Your Medical Care

Do you want your soon-to-be ex-wife to have the right to terminate life support if you're sick and unable to make a decision? Hardly. The living wills or healthcare proxies that you signed naming your wife as the primary person (agent) to make medical and healthcare decisions are still effective until you change them. Living wills are legal documents stating your healthcare preferences. Healthcare proxies appoint an agent to address healthcare matters for you. If you fall ill after separation, but before the final decree of divorce, your wife is likely the person named to make medical decisions. If you're injured in a car accident, the doctors will call the wife you just separated from to ask whether they should pull the plug. So revise your living wills and healthcare proxies and cancel the old ones!

Rule #37. Make Sure Your Wife Will Not Inherit Everything You Have

If you were to die unexpectedly before your divorce is final, would you want your intended ex to get all your assets? Would you want her to be in charge of your estate? It's unlikely that you would want either of these scenarios to happen. You may have suffered through six horrible months of divorce settlement negotiations read 32 drafts of legal documents, and everyone may plan to sign the final papers next week. But if you die before signing, your wife might get everything.*

The answer is to revise your will (or if you haven't signed one, go to an attorney specializing in estate planning and get one). Your will should state who should be the executor. If you have children, consider setting up trusts for them and naming people you trust to be trustees (they will manage and distribute money as trustees). If you have a revocable living trust, be sure to update it as well.

Although you might want to leave nothing to your ex-wife, the laws of most states won't permit that but require that you designate some minimum amount for your spouse. If you fail to do so, then your spouse will have the right to elect to get a portion of your estate. In many states, this is one-third of your assets. So be very careful. The laws differ considerably from state to state. You must consult with an estate attorney in your state to find out the rules and how to protect your assets. Once you negotiate a final divorce agreement, the terms of that agreement will likely dictate what your spouse is entitled to. Exhibit 2.1 shows a sample disinheritance clause your attorney can adapt for your will.

Although the will you sign now may have to be changed to reflect the terms of the final divorce agreement, don't put off signing a new will (and revocable living trust). Just remember to take your final divorce agreement to your estate planner so that he or she can help update your estate planning documents to reflect any requirements you must meet.

---

*For more information on estate planning and divorce see: Shenkman, *The Complete Book of Trusts* (2nd ed) (John Wiley & Sons, Inc. 1999).

Rule #37. Make Sure Your Wife Will Not Inherit

No Bequest.

I intentionally make no bequest to my spouse, [Spouse Name] (herein "my spouse"), who is presently my spouse and whom I am in the process of divorcing.

Distributions Required Pursuant
to any Divorce or Separation Agreement.

If a legally binding settlement agreement governs my spouse's property rights and interests in my estate has been executed, I direct my Executor to honor any payments or obligations which I may have under said Agreement. I similarly direct my Executor to reasonably pursue any rights which I may have under said Agreement.

Spousal Right of Election.

If, and only if, at the time of my death: (i) no binding settlement agreement governing my spouse's property rights and interests in my estate has been executed; (ii) my spouse is legally entitled to make a right of election against my estate notwithstanding my disinheritance of her above; and (iii) if she exercises such right of election under applicable [insert your state name] law as a surviving spouse, then and only then, shall the bequest in the following paragraph be made.

If my spouse survives me, and is at the time of my death legally my spouse and she is entitled to an elective share under [Reference to your state law here] and if my spouse exercises her right to claim an elective share, then and only then, I give, devise and bequeath to my spouse the amount which is necessary so that the value of assets passing to my spouse equals the minimum amount which my spouse is entitled to pursuant to the statutory right of election provided under the applicable [Your state name] law.

Exhibit 2.1   Intentional disinheritance of spouse.

Rule #38. Consider Disclaiming Your Inheritance

If you're about to get divorced, or in the midst of a divorce, consider "disclaiming" any assets you inherit. A disclaimer is a process by which you file a legal document in court stating that you don't want the assets that someone (e.g., your parents) left you under their will. The assets will then pass to someone else, but you should have an experienced estate planner help you determine exactly where before he or she helps you disclaim. The someone else may be your sister, whom you would rather have the assets than your soon-to-be ex-wife.

3

What You Need to Know before You Leave Home

Rule #39. Don't Leave the House until Your Lawyer Says You Should

If you move out of the marital residence, you may provide your wife with a substantial financial advantage: she can reside in the residence, and you will increase your personal expenses with rental costs and other living expenses. Moving out may also make it much harder for you to protect your financial interest in the house. Your wife may then, depending on the facts, be able to get a court order barring you from the premises. You won't even be able to get back your tennis racket unless you get a court order. Also, keep in mind that getting a court order costs money because the attorneys' clocks (hers and yours) are running.

Furthermore, your wife may claim that you have abandoned your children if you move out of the house. Depending on your state law and the facts in your case, this could be serious. In other situations, moving out may not matter: in some states, the law will not infer abandonment if you have been and remain a committed and involved father. Finally, in some situations, you should never move out of the house if you're seeking custody, because you're leaving the child.

If you're the primary breadwinner, you should not move out of the house unless your presence in the house triggers domestic violence issues, encourages your wife to file a complaint, or makes the living situation worse for your children. The best interests of your children should always supersede other considerations. If you move out, you're supporting two households and fix the temporary support *(pendente lite)* obligation to your wife prior to divorce. You fix a temporary support order by moving out. This increases your financial burden. It shows dependency, it establishes need on the part of your wife and gives her a better argument for support. It may also take the pressure off your wife to move toward a settlement. If your wife is successful in obtaining a high temporary support order, your relocation may make it more difficult to resolve the case, cautions Lynne Strober, Esq., of Mandelbaum, Salsburg, Gold, Lazris, Discenza & Steinberg, in West Orange, New Jersey.

Another warning: don't let your emotions overcome common sense. For example, if you move out and end up in a one-room apartment, you may be embarrassed to bring your children over for their birthdays or holidays. A small and inadequate apartment may not provide a place for your kids to spend the night.

Rule #40. Plan Ahead before You Move

If you know several years before filing for divorce that your marriage is on the rocks, take appropriate steps to avoid commingling your financial accounts. For instance, if you are receiving annual bonuses or rental income on property you own solely, set up individual accounts. These records can help confirm the separate nature of gift, inheritance, or other property.

If you are planning on moving out, alert all the utility companies about removing your name on the forthcoming bills.

Rule #41. Line Up Experts to Help You in Your Divorce

A key to successfully navigating the divorce process is having a good team of experts. As discussed in Chapter 2, you can't navigate the legal minefields without a good matrimonial attorney. An accountant may also be essential for ferreting out assets your wife hides, interpreting expense data, and cautioning you about tax return problems. And the best solution for custody and visitation disputes is a trained therapist. The court is not the best place to resolve issues relating to the children. A good therapist can mediate and assist in establishing visitation.

Get these professionals involved before you move out. Once you've moved, you may not have access to data the accountant wants and may have sacrificed important legal rights. And if the move and steps leading up to it aren't handled properly, you may cause avoidable difficulties for the children. So get your advisers in place first.

Rule #42. Be Certain You Have a Nest Egg in Your Name

Professionals (doctors, accountants, etc.) often transfer most or all of their assets to their spouse to avoid malpractice and other claims. This is not an ideal approach because in the event of a divorce, even in states where "equitable distribution" should divide your assets without regard to whose name they are in, there may be a lengthy period before you can access them.

A preferable approach would be to retain some assets in your name. If you are still concerned about malpractice or other risks, consider forming a domestic asset protection trust in either Alaska or Delaware to hold assets. This will enable you to transfer assets where your creditors cannot reach them (assuming there is no fraudulent conveyance in the transfer), but you can remain a discretionary beneficiary of the trustee. Also, use irrevocable trusts, S corporations, family limited partnerships, and other techniques that enable you to access assets while minimizing the risk of a creditor or malpractice claimant reaching your assets.

Consider other sources of funding your living expenses and professional fees while the divorce is proceeding. Home equity lines, if you are still able to access them, can help. Personal lines of credit, if they were in place, can also be used. And although they are perhaps the worst choice, if there are no others, you can use credit cards.

Rule #43. Cut up Credit Cards with Your Wife's Name

Avoid the risk of your ex running up large bills prior to her leaving or throwing you out. You don't want your wife to max out all credit limits on your joint credit cards before the split occurs, leaving you jointly liable for the debts and affecting your credit record negatively. Credit cards are often joint obligations of both you and your wife. If your ex used credit cards, even without your knowledge and consent, and even if in violation of a separation agreement, you're possibly still jointly liable and are jointly obligated to pay debt she incurred.

Rule #43. Cut up Credit Cards with Your Wife's Name

Even if the credit card is in your name only, you may simply have obtained an additional card for your wife. If your ex goes out and runs up thousands of dollars in expenses before the divorce and walks away, she has no liability; her name is not on the account, even though she spent it all. The bank will only go after you.

This type of problem is real. One husband found this out the hard way seven full years after the divorce, and long after he thought he could quit worrying about his ex! "The husband and his new wife applied for a home loan and were turned down. Flabbergasted, he obtained a credit report. To his shock and dismay there was a large write-off three years earlier by a credit card company," explains Ginita Wall, an accountant in San Diego. "The husband eventually found out that his ex-wife had run up large bills on a joint credit card and then declared bankruptcy. The bankruptcy absolved her from repaying the credit card company even though the divorce decree had specifically obligated her to pay it!"

A practical tip that can help many couples is for you and your ex to take out separate credit cards. Then transfer to the new separate cards the portion of the balance from the joint cards you each agreed to assume responsibility for. This will avoid the joint liability problem.

About the only exception to the credit card horror stories is if your wife forged your signature. Even if these charges should fairly be charged against the settlement your ex receives, many people getting divorced have no assets. In the worst cases, the credit card debt could cause you to file bankruptcy.

If you think divorce is imminent, the solution to this problem is to cancel all your credit cards to ensure that they can't be abused. "When the trust begins to fade, cancel the credit cards," cautions Colleen A. Brown, Esq., partner in Lawrence, Werner, Kesselring, Swartout & Brown, LLP, in Canandaigua, New York.

On the other hand, think twice before following the preceding advice. It's right for some but definitely not for all. Destroying your wife's access to credit in other situations may actually be a spiteful and counterproductive step. If your wife won't act irresponsibly, the two of you can cooperate for everyone's benefit. If your wife is financially strapped and an attorney is egging her on, cutting off her access to credit cards may play right into the game, exacerbating the entire divorce process.

Ideally, your wife should have credit cards in her own name. This will also facilitate her establishing credit and getting on her feet financially after the divorce. Any help you can render to her in that regard while you are still married will make it easier for everybody later. If all the cards are in your name, use your business contacts to help her get a personal loan and credit card in her name. Ask banks where you have business contacts to extend your wife a line of credit, personal loan, and credit card. This will help her build a credit history, give her more financial experience if she didn't have it before, and help her become more self-confident. All of this can help everyone involved. If your actions demonstrate that you're not trying to pull the rug out from under your ex, and if you can help her gain confidence financially, she's less apt to fall prey to a vindictive divorce process. Helping your soon-to-be ex build financial confidence and security will make her more independent and help you both move more quickly into your new lives.

Rule #44. Take a Picture of Every Asset You Own

A picture can truly be worth a thousand words. So photograph . . . photograph . . . everything! Photograph (and preferably videotape) your marital home, any furnishings, artwork, jewelry, or other assets that could corroborate your position with respect to the divorce property settlement. Make a detailed list of assets and their values. Don't overlook disclosing anything that could otherwise be identified. If you're caught, hiding assets will destroy any credibility you had. Assume that your wife has probably done the same: videotaped and photocopied any records that she even remotely had access to.

Eventually, you will need to compile a detailed list of all marital assets. The photographs you take, lists you make, and documents you photocopy before you move out will be invaluable.

Photographs can often have ancillary unexpected uses. For example, if your wife claims in the court papers she files that she needs an allowance for clothing, a photograph of a closet stuffed with clothing may work wonders on reducing or eliminating the unnecessary request. If your spouse has a 14' × 18' closet packed full of clothes and shoes, your lawyer might make a case when setting up alimony payments that a clothing allowance is uncalled for.

Weed out unnecessary assets that can create valuation issues or other problems later. If you own a boat that your spouse doesn't care for, her lawyer might make a case that it's worth "X," when in reality it's worth 20 percent less. So get rid of it: convert it to cash. No one can argue the value of cash. Take a look at everything on your list and price it fairly. Use blue book values on vehicles; have other items appraised independently when necessary. Know what you have to settle with. Decide what you will need from the marital assets to set up separate living accommodations. Be careful when selecting which assets you want: unless there are duplicates, one of you may need to replace them with new. For kids, having familiar items in each home is reassuring. The best approach is for you and your ex to jointly decide who gets what assets, if you can agree.

Rule #45. Safeguard Important Data on a Backup Computer Disk

If a picture is worth a thousand words, a diskette of computer files may be worth a million! Therefore, you should copy any computer files that have financial, legal, and similar data on a diskette or a Zip drive and store it in a secure place. This can prevent your ex from destroying valuable data in a fit of anger. It will also likely include much of the data your attorney will need to help you on your case.

If you have data your ex shouldn't see (e.g., romantic e-mails to your cyberlover), do more than delete them. "Deleted files can often be recovered by a computer consultant," cautions Ginita Wall, an accountant in San Diego. "This could make for some interesting reading for your ex, and some rather embarrassing disclosures for you."

Want to be a good Joe and demonstrate your reasonableness? Give your wife a computer diskette for her lawyer of your accounting or checkbook program. This will include all the data in an easily usable format and could save lots of hours of professional fees.

Rule #46. Minimize or Eliminate Your Wife's Involvement with Your Business

In a recent divorce case of considerable notoriety, Gary Wendt, the former CEO of GE Capital concluded a divorce with his wife of many years. She argued (quite persuasively, as the settlement demonstrated), that she has been very involved in his business. She hosted many dinner parties for her husband and his colleagues. She traveled regularly with him on his business trips throughout the United States and the world. And she therefore was given a $20,000,000 settlement as reported by the media and now under appeal. So if divorce is likely, reduce or eliminate your wife's involvement in your business to minimize such claims.

If your business is closely held, your wife's involvement creates a second risk. Involvement in a limited capacity (as opposed to a full-time active partner) could allow her to sleuth out information about the business and lead her to draw inappropriate conclusions about the profitability of the business or other financial arrangements. For example, if you purchased flowers for your home on one or two occasions and the charges were accidentally billed to the business, she may erroneously conclude that you routinely bill personal expenses to the business.

As with all the recommendations in this book, don't act without thinking everything through the whole way. If your wife is gainfully employed in your business and earning a salary, what will you accomplish by cutting her out? Also, in most cases the actions described previously are simply too late. If your wife has been the consummate "Boss's wife" for decades, cutting her out of the picture six months before the divorce won't change the facts of her contribution, it will probably make it look as if you were preparing for divorce by cutting her out. Funny, that's exactly what you were doing! For any of these "strategies," you face risks of backlash that can be far worse than the problem you were trying to address. Worse, if there was a chance of minimizing the adversarial and combative nature of the divorce process, these acts might incite vengeance, which wouldn't be particularly productive.

Rule #47. Try to Stay on Good Terms with Your In-Laws

If you are on good terms with your in-laws, see them before filing for divorce and explain the situation, even though they probably already know from your wife. Even ask your sister-in-law to come down to your house and be at your wife's side when your wife interviews lawyers. Show consideration; you don't need any more enemies. Remember, this is an emotional roller coaster, and although you are honest and ethical, your wife's family may *not* be objective. Nevertheless, anything you can do to keep things peaceful and above board is beneficial.

Rule #48. Get a Post Office Box

Before you leave the marital home, begin rerouting all your mail to a post office box. This can avoid the difficulties of having to negotiate to get your mail and prevents your wife from having access to your confidential records or documents. This does not mean to hide assets or income by routing mail through a post office box. In most cases, your wife's attorney or forensic accountant will discover the income and assets and you'll lose any credibility.

Even if your wife is cooperative in the divorce process, there's another benefit: your address may not be permanent for a number of years. It's a lot easier to retrieve mail from a single box address for a couple of years than to keeping notifying everyone of a new address.

Rule #48. Get a Post Office Box

A post office box can be helpful as long as you don't misuse it! If you receive financial and other information for marital assets at your post office box, you must fully report and disclose this information. Your use of a post office box does not minimize your responsibility to maintain marital assets. The safest approach is to route primarily separate property and personal correspondence to the post office box.

4

Communicating with Your Children

Rule #49. Prepare for the Pain of Missing Your Children

Contrary to the "bad dad" myths, most divorced dads love their kids and try to be good fathers. Most problems arise because of a rancorous divorce process or because the ex-wife turns the kids off from their father, making it difficult or impossible for the father to continue a relationship. Many divorced dads feel as if they were kicked out of their kids' lives. Yet the "bad dad" myth prevails. This myth has resulted in laws and a system which in many cases favors the wife unfairly in terms of custody and child support. This shouldn't happen, but too often it does. So prepare yourself for the heartache; if you're emotionally prepared, you'll fare better.

Rule #50. Try to Keep Anger out of the Divorce Process, for the Sake of Your Children

"If you want to screw up your kids, have an angry divorce," warns Lynne Gold-Bikin of the Norristown, Pennsylvania, law firm Wolf, Block, Schorr & Solis-Cohen. Have a custody fight. Don't pay your child support. Use your kids as message carriers (e.g., "You tell your mother that if she doesn't do such and such I won't send a check"). Use the kids as spies ("What did your mom do with . . ."). As much as men say women do this, men do it just as often. Ask any kid in America whose parents are divorced what they want and they'll say they want their parents back together again and not to fight. Never denigrate their mother to them.

Any parents who love their kids will admit that the worst part of a divorce is not seeing their kids. So when negotiating custody, close your eyes and try to feel you have the same visitation schedule you're trying to make your spouse understand. The kids are the bottom line. Practically, if you work to 10 P.M. every night and you have not been actively parenting, what are you going to be able to do for your kids? Even if your wife is being really difficult, it doesn't make it better for your kids for you to be nasty too. It's in the best interest of your children to have access to both parents, so try to work out a schedule that works for all of you.

Rule #51. Try Not to Damage Your Children

There is a lot of misinformation about divorce and its impact on children. "You're not necessarily condemning your kids to a life of misery by divorcing," observes Dr. Kenneth N. Condrell, a child psychologist and family counselor and the author of *Be a Great Divorced Dad* (St. Martin's Press, 1998). The divorce itself does not have to damage the children as people once believed. What is critical is how the parents—you and your ex—behave during and after the divorce. If the children lose access to close relatives (e.g., grandparents, aunts, or uncles) as a result of the divorce, because of anger or parental fighting, this loss is detrimental. If you or your ex continually pressure the children to take sides against the other parent, they will be very stressed. If your children become alienated from either parent because you and your ex refuse to have anything to do with each other, they will suffer considerably. If the parents continue to fight in front of the kids, the negative impact grows. Therefore, you and your ex should avoid or prevent all these situations.

What children handle divorce relatively well? The kids who do well continue to see grandma and grandpa, and mom and dad keep their fighting private and don't ruin the relationship the children have with the other parent. These kids are not likely to become emotionally disturbed, but there is a heartache that the kids will carry for their entire lives. It is something they will feel sad about and regret. It never really goes away. This, however, is not necessarily harmful to the child's growth and maturity.

What about the Wallerstein studies which found that divorce is so emotionally damaging to children and that are quoted all the time? These studies implied substantial harm to children of divorce for decades afterward. These studies are flawed, notes Dr. Condrell. The people quoting Wallerstein generally don't identify the sources of the study data. The subjects in the study were people who were already patients in clinics. They were families who already had significant personal problems, so her study was skewed. Wallerstein is on target in stating that it takes at least five years for a family to get reestablished after a divorce emotionally. After only one year, most families are still facing anger, conflict, and unresolved issues, so although divorce is supposed to be a fresh start, the first year or so will not provide this.

Rule #52. Explain Everything to Your Children

To minimize the negative effect of divorce on your children, make a pact with your wife to tell the children together. Divorce is often riddled with anger and miscommunication. Informing the children together (before one of you leaves the marital home) helps reduce speculation during and after the divorce. It is also harder for either of you to get caught up in blaming the other when you start out by informing the children together.

If you don't inform your children fully and consistently, they will "fill in the blanks" of what they don't understand with their own interpretations, thoughts, worries, and sometimes nightmares. Minimize this risk. Talk to your children and tell them as much as is appropriate.

Addressing the divorce issues with your children is often critical to helping them through the trauma of divorce. Don't ignore their fears, worries, and concerns. If you are not already in counseling, the best approach is to consult with a therapist and discuss the situation thoroughly. Work out a plan to best help the children and stick with it. Coordinate everything with your wife. It will be hard enough on the children without you and your wife saying different things to confuse them more. Never play "good cop/bad cop" with the children. Don't blame your wife in front of them. Encourage her not to blame you in front of them either. Don't criticize your wife in front of the children. Encourage her not to criticize you in front of them either. The harm and anguish you cause your children by speaking badly about their mother to them can be incalculable. It could easily backfire and hurt your relationship with them. It will assuredly weigh against you in any custody or other court proceeding. The approach should be as positive as possible.

Rule #53. Adapt Your Explanations to Each Child's Age and Maturity

"You must tell the child. But the communication must be tailored to the developmental level of the individual child. You don't tell a three-year-old that you're splitting up because Mommy had an affair," warns Janet Andron Hoffman, EdD, LCSW, in Teaneck, New Jersey. Before you sit down with your child, you must have a game plan. You must remain the adult. You can't look to the child to parent you.

Each child will react differently depending on his or her particular temperament. You must think about how you will talk to each of them at their respective individual levels. Here are some guidelines:

Infants and Toddlers (under 3 years old). You must be clear and succinct. For example, you might say something like, "Daddy is not going to be living in the house, but Daddy will come every day after dinnertime." You must also be specific. The child may not understand immediately, so you will have to repeat yourself over and over. Because cognitively they may not understand, they may show all sorts of symptoms: they could start crying or regress in toilet training. Children under 3 years old have particular difficulty with transitions (e.g., going to daycare, switching between parents). They don't understand that Daddy or Mommy is coming back. So reassure them as often as possible—for example, you might say something like "Daddy and Mommy may be fighting, but we both love you very much." How your child reacts to your divorce also depends on what your child witnessed. Also, joint custody can be very hard on the child at this young age. There are

63

all sorts of different custody configurations, so try to coordinate with your ex-wife and be thoughtful in working out a visitation agreement. Custody should not be a battleground for what's best for either spouse. For a child this young, however, it's best to primarily be with one parent for stability.

Ages 3 to 5 (Preschoolers). Emphasize that Mommy and Daddy aren't getting along and will live separately, but Daddy will see the child often. The child will ask when, so you must know what the arrangement will be before you tell your child about the divorce. Emphasize that both of you love your child and that you'll both be there to care for your child. Compassion and sensitivity are especially important for this age because the child is likely to feel responsible for the split-up.

Ages 6 to 11 (School Age). Be clear about what the child may have noticed. For example, seeing mommy and daddy fight or cry can have a significant and negative impact on your child. Therefore, you should encourage your children to express their feelings because divorce is a tragedy for the family. Ask your child, "If you've been missing Mommy or Daddy, do you want to talk about it?" Encourage your children to call their mother when they are visiting with you, and encourage your ex to reciprocate.

Preteens and Teens. You must really communicate, be direct and tell them what is going on.

Rule #54. Maintain Ongoing Communications and Contact with Your Children

Be sure to keep communication ongoing. Your child may think "What did I do wrong that made Daddy hate me?" Or your child may ask, "Mommy, what did you do wrong that made Daddy hate me?" Fathers play a pivotal role in their children's development and when a father is not there, it takes a toll on the kids.

"The legal system is absurd. It doesn't recognize that Daddy has to see his kids," asserts Janet Andron Hoffman, EdD, LCSW, in Teaneck, New Jersey. So call your child every day, send tapes of you talking or telling a story, and write letters and stay on top of what the child is doing. You need to be there. The more parents are involved with a child's education, the more successful the child will be. Also, maintain a consistent environment. Anticipate what your children will need in terms of clothing, school supplies, and personal effects. This may be confusing, so make sure you work it out with your wife. Both parents have to get copies of the report card, notification of school events, plays, and so forth. Parents must sit down with the school personnel and advise them that there are now two households.

You don't want your children to play one parent off the other for gifts. So don't buy your children's love. You must resist this. Gifts are not a substitute for the open communication discussed above. Keep your children's needs first. Discipline consistently. Put aside your hatred and pain and look at the kids who are falling apart and see what you can do to make it better for the child. In the schools, different visitations may see kids "flipping out" after being at one parent's.

Reassurance is the common theme. Stability, consistency, and routine are key, even though the rug has been pulled out from under the child. This is especially hard if you have to relocate and go merely for visitation. The problem is that visitation can be awkward and artificial for the child, but you can make it work.

Rule #55. Prevent Your Ex from Turning the Children against You

Contrary to the "bad dad" myth a good relationship between a father and child is important to any child's development. A recent study by the National Center on Addiction and Substance Abuse at Columbia University found that teenagers who don't get along with their dads are 68 percent more likely to smoke, drink, and use drugs than teens living in a two parent household. There are lots more horrible statistics.

Many ex-wives still undermine the father's relationship with the children. Because the father is generally the one who leaves the home, children can read into this that he has abandoned them. If your ex is really concerned about the well-being of your children, she should make efforts to assure the children that the fact that you moved out doesn't mean that you've divorced the children or don't love them. This often doesn't happen. Your moving out puts the kids in the preserve of the mother full time. If your ex is angry or vengeful, she can feed them bad information about you. For example, your ex might abuse the circumstances and say things like "your father has left us and doesn't love us," and this can turn the children against you.

What can you as a father do? If you're smart, don't make it worse for yourself by moving in with another woman too quickly. So much damage comes from this that kids won't forget the pain you caused. Kids need time to process the divorce and all of the trauma they've experienced. If you compress their acclimation time by moving in with a new woman within a few weeks or months, it will be extraordinarily difficult to maintain a good relationship with your children. If you have someone new, be discreet: your kids simply cannot handle a divorce and a new woman in your life all at one time. By nature, kids are very loyal to their mothers, and they will interpret your new relationship as being bad for mom, especially if mom is home crying all the time.

Most important, you must show your children love. Be a reliable dad who sees his kids regularly. "Prove by your actions that you will be there for them. Help them understand that there will be a different kind of family, but a family nevertheless," encourages Dr. Condrell.

How can you demonstrate to a court that your ex is turning your children against you? Make tape recordings (after asking your lawyer for instructions and limitations), save e-mails, and keep a log of incidents.

Rule #56. Play Smart to Get More Time with Your Children

If you want custody of your kids, play it smart. Make sure you know the names of your child's best friends, when your child sees the dentist, and other important information. Go to every parent/teacher conference, get involved in your child's activities. To the extent possible, take your child to doctor appointments and provide primary care. Make decisions related to school matters. Speak to school officials about any issues and problems confronting your child. Call the school and get put on the mailing list so that you will know when school events occur.

Spend your free time with your child. "Treat the child as the primary person in your life," recommends Lynne Strober, Esq., of Mandelbaum, Salsburg, Gold, Lazris, Discenza & Steinberg in West Orange, New Jersey. Have as many people as possible who could be good witnesses observe your close relationship with your child. Document and corroborate this relationship.

Rule #57. Establish an Appropriate Visitation Arrangement

The typical arrangement is every other weekend and one midweek visit. For some children, say a younger child, this can be hard. Sending a toddler away from mommy may be terrible, so it may be better to go to dinner a few nights a week instead of having your young children overnight. Start like this and move into overnight as the child feels comfortable.

Are these "typical" arrangements appropriate? "Set formulas are stupid, it's not in keeping with the child's needs," asserts Janet Andron Hoffman, EdD, LCSW, a child therapist in Teaneck, New Jersey. These schedules are often simply not enough time for a child who really needs to be with his or her dad. The parents have to be open. There should be room for some flexibility but on the other hand, you don't want to lose consistency. Also, what is right for one child may not be right for another child. As children grow up, the schedule should also change as their needs, maturity, and understanding change.

"Seeing a father one night a week for dinner is outrageous!" says Hoffman. If you can't see your children because of an unreasonable ex or because of what the court determined, then at least call your children, e-mail them, send them tapes with your voice, read them stories on tapes, anything to stay in touch and remind them that you care. The separation and divorce agreements should include potential for reevaluation and adjustment of the visitation schedule as the child grows. The typical stringent agreements that are so common (against you, the dad), which are too often negotiated "with the kids being bartered for like property, assures that the kids will get screwed up," Hoffman notes.

Rule #58. Consider Different Types of Custody

The names may differ depending on the state, but whatever the terminology, the custody arrangement is key to determining the amount of child support you pay, the time you have with your children, and the input you will have on major decisions affecting their lives.

Joint legal custody means you and your ex share in decision making. This does not mean that you have joint *physical* custody. Physical custody arrangements can differ from legal custody arrangements. In joint legal custody, both parents have the right to carry out the custodial duties of parenthood; that is, you share in decisions regarding elective surgery and other health issues, school selection and other education decisions, and the general welfare of your children. To obtain joint legal custody, you may have to show the court that you're capable of compromise. You must demonstrate that you can communicate and compromise and not just argue. You should endeavor to solve the problems together, not through your lawyers' negotiating, or a judge dictating. "Unfortunately, this doesn't happen enough because couples often start out with game playing, then it becomes a matter of winning, and winning requires confrontation, and there is no winner in a confrontation, especially the children," says Barry Croland, Esq., Shapiro & Croland, Hackensack, New Jersey.

Because Texas has a no-fault divorce, joint legal custody is relatively easy to get. "It's favorable for fathers for joint custody, it's presumed that fathers should have joint custody," notes Robert E. Holmes, Jr., Esq., of Holmes, Woods & Garza, in Dallas, Texas.

Joint physical custody is hard, but you can come closer to a 50/50 custody arrangement if both you and your ex live in the same state and close enough to each other that school and other arrangements can be worked out. A typical arrangement could also include unequal divisions in the summer, such as two weeks to a month at a time. Another common arrangement is alternating weekends, and perhaps one or several overnight visits during the off week. Holidays typically alternate. People who fight for this time forget sometimes that they want time for themselves, especially if they have other children. Many women have agreed to fathers having the children Friday after school through Sunday night. Some fathers ask for Thursday nights through Sunday or Monday school if school arrangements can be worked out. "Fathers as a whole are spending more time to be involved with their children," says David L. Levy. "That's great for the kids."

Rule #58. Consider Different Types of Custody

The primary residential parent has the right to make more major decisions. Unfortunately for most men, the mother is typically designated as the primary residential parent and you, the father, are allotted visitation or parenting time. This will be weekend visits, and so forth.

The right type of custody arrangement is "both parents," asserts David L. Levy, Esq., cofounder and President Children's Rights Council in Washington, D.C. Children with two parents in their lives have a much better chance of avoiding problems and will have better academic performance. The typical visitation arrangement with the father seeing his kids one night during the week and every other weekend is just not enough. Shared parenting and joint custody is the best approach. This means shared decision making on major decisions. Even more important than shared legal parenting is joint physical custody, where each parent has the child at least one-third of the time. This is the minimum most experts believe is necessary for parents to have a healthy relationship with their children. Visitation of every other weekend usually only amounts to about 15 percent of the total time. The trend is moving in the direction of shared parenting. You can have a variety of arrangements to best meet the needs of the child. If parents live in the same school district, this should be easy to arrange. Many psychologist favor the shared approach. It's often the adults who have the problem with shared parenting, not the child. If the adults can handle this type of arrangement maturely, the child can thrive. Substitute mediation for an adversarial legal proceeding to enhance your chance of working out a better custody arrangement. Children's rights groups can help fathers better understand how to help their children through the divorce process by informing and educating them, suggests David Levy. To get a directory of children's rights groups listing over

1,000 groups all over the country, call Paul Robinson, editor *Children's Rights Council Parenting Directory* (202–547-6227; book or diskette, $15.00; or $12.00 for members).

Rule #59. Understand How Your Custody Arrangement May Influence Your Child Support Payments

The amount you pay may be affected by how many overnight visits you have with your children. Although your child's interests must come first, the number of overnight visitations you have may reduce the child support payment to your ex. This may provide yet another incentive for how you negotiate the structure of parenting time, suggests Lynne Strober, Esq., of Mandelbaum, Salsburg, Gold, Lazris, Discenza & Steinberg, in West Orange, New Jersey. "I haven't had a father that hasn't complained about how child support is handled. It's understandable," says Paul L. Feinstein, Esq., of Chicago, Illinois. In Illinois, the mother doesn't have to account for the child support money. Part of the reason for this is a federal plan of mandated state support guidelines; you have a cookie cutter approach that the father is required to pay a set percentage of his income to the mother. This is not always fair, because there is less flexibility in allocating who pays what. The rationale for all of this is that the feds were most worried about "deadbeat dads." That doesn't make for a great system, nor does it address the myriad other issues and inequities created. It's just another reflection of how the "bad dad" myth has taken hold of the divorce system.

Rule #60. Express Your Emotions

Don't be afraid to express your sadness about the divorce. Hang in there when your child rebuffs you. Don't walk away. Put your ego in your pocket and try to be there for the kids. Remember that you are a role model for your child, who will look to you to see how you handle conflict resolution, stress, and anger. These messages are subtle, but the kids pick up on them.

Rule #61. Handle Visits with Your Children Properly

Be diligent to maintain a strong bond with your children. Call before every visit. Be punctual when plans are made. Try to center activities around the children's interests. Activities don't have to be Disneyland every week. Try to enjoy normal or regular activities. Don't be unnatural. Don't try to make every visit a special activity. Kids will enjoy quiet activities such as building a model, playing a game, or even cooking dinner with you.

Rule #62. Remain Civil to Your Ex-Wife

"For kids to feel whole, they have to feel good about both parents. You must encourage their relationship with your ex even if you can't stand her. You must encourage your kids to have a close relationship if you care about them, this is the most loving thing you can do for them," notes Michele Weiner-Davis.

Hostility toward your ex-wife—no matter how angry you feel, no matter how certain you are that she "deserves it"—will only create tension and difficulty for your children. No child can benefit from being in the middle of tension or fights between parents. Better yet, try to show consistency in dealings with the children. If you and your ex can agree on discipline and show consistency and uniformity on everything from your children's dating to their school attendance and manners, it will be far easier on your children. It will also improve and preserve your relationship with them.

Rule #63. Keep a Log of Visitation

Keep detailed records of the days and times you are supposed to visit with, or speak to, your children and the actual days and times you see or speak with them. If it becomes necessary, these records can later demonstrate that your ex-wife is trying to alienate you, suggests Amy J. Amundsen, Esq., of Memphis, Tennessee.

Rule #64. Develop a Better Relationship with Your Children

Listen to your children more than ever. Hear their concerns and respond accordingly. Whenever feasible and to the extent their ages permit, let them become involved in making decisions that affect them. This is especially important for preteens and teens. These children are relatively mature and you must give them some choices or you will infantalize them. You can't tell them where to be and when. The child may want to spend more time with one parent than the other. Adolescence is such a roller coaster time anyway. Sexual feelings are developing. Your divorce may magnify the emotional difficulties of the teenage years. Children given choices handle the divorce better. What visitation schedules would they like? What do they want to do during a visit? At which home do they want to leave which of their toys? The mental anguish they confront can be enormous. The divorcing spouses consult their children too seldom about their preferences. Live with dad, live with mom? When can they see the nonresident spouse, and so on. While the judge might ask children for their opinions, kids are wrapped up in emotion and frightened by the courtroom setting. Don't attempt to pit your kids against one another, but try to settle child-related differences between you and your ex before entering the courtroom. This is a very emotional time for most children—divorce is of your doing—not theirs. Take the gloves off long enough to listen to their needs. You're jointly responsible for them, forever—even though divorce carries you permanently apart.

Rule #65. Never Use Your Children to Get What You Want

Your obligations as a father don't end. Your love for your children shouldn't either. Never use children as a weapon in divorce. Never barter arrangements with your children for issue with your ex. For example, Christmas this year is your turn to have the children. Your ex is complaining about some financial matter and threatening to call her lawyer. Don't trade her ignoring the financial matter for her getting the kids for Christmas.

Rule #66. Give Your Children Time to Discover the Real You

"The deck is stacked against men when it comes to the children. You have to be careful how you handle yourself," says Dr. Condrell, a child psychologist and family counselor, author of *Be a Great Divorced Dad.*

Fathers in unhappy marriages don't always have the best relationship with their kids. They can be irritable, argue with their wives, and not be around. After the divorce, your kids may discover that you are more fun and more relaxed. So be patient with your kids and let them see what you are all about outside this bad marriage. If your kids aren't receptive right away, give it time. Let them see who you really are.

Rule #67. Keep Your Children in Touch with Relatives

Encourage them to see relatives even if the relatives dislike you. Help the kids honor them with their birthdays and so on. If you badmouth your ex-wife's relatives, you're only shooting yourself in the foot.

Rule #68. Give Your Children Permission to Love Mom's New Partner

Divorce is a fresh start and mom will sooner or later have a new companion. Many fathers cannot handle the fact that their children are in the presence of another man. This puts the kids in a terrible bind. You should take comfort that you're their only dad and will always be special. The presence of another man can help your children if you can help them make it work. Kids can get into a loyalty conflict. They may think, "if I like mom's friend, I'm hurting dad." Give them permission to like and have fun with mom's new friend. If you don't, your kids will be distant and will probably hide their true feelings from you. They will start playing games to keep you from knowing that your ex-wife is involved with someone new. Having to lie or hide important relationships creates considerable stress. They feel as if they are doing something bad. Don't put your children in that position, no matter how angry and hurt you are about your ex-wife's new friend.

Rule #69. Be a Reliable Dad about Seeing Your Children

Because you probably left the marital home, your kids' biggest concern is that you abandoned them and don't care about them. So make sure you have a schedule to be with them and that you honor that schedule. Don't break plans at the last minute. This will make the kids mistrustful. If you want to build closeness, you must see them regularly. Dads can pretty much be over a barrel if the mother won't let them visit. If this happens, you may experience parental alienation syndrome, where the wife tries to destroy the relationship with the father. In this situation, your only remedy may be court. The court may order counseling.

You cannot make teenagers visit as easily. Sometimes you may wonder if the kid doesn't want to come or if the mom is influencing the kid. When the kid has been brainwashed by the mother, however, his or her behavior is obvious. How do you know if your child is alienated? Most children are ambivalent in their feelings toward both parents after a divorce, but an alienated child has strong one-sided emotions about the dad: Feelings are not mixed, just all bad. When they make excuses, it sounds like you've pressed a button on a recording. They've been through it so many times with their mother, your ex, they just keep repeating the same story that is supposed to justify their position. You may feel like you cannot win with this child: If you don't call, they think you don't care; if you do call, they think you're harassing them. If you send a present, they think you're trying to buy them; if you don't send a present, they think you don't love them. If this happens, get a psychologist to interview the child as a "friend of the court" and make recommendations as to what steps you should take, and to what extent the court should get involved to influence the mother's actions.

Mommy has more power than dad and can play on it. For the most part mother's have a special bond with the kids and she is the one the kids are living with. In the eyes of the kids she is the weaker parent (kids usually perceive the mother as the weaker one even if she is not) and they will sympathize with the mother. So mothers have an edge.

Rule #70. Don't Sue for Sole Custody to Get a Better Financial Package

Men are sometimes advised to do this, but this often only makes the situation worse. There has been some improvement in the lot of fathers, but it's only a small step. There continues to be a bias in the courts against men.

Moreover, getting your children from Friday evening to Saturday evening isn't how to define a weekend. A weekend should be Friday after school until Monday morning. You really need enough days to have the children get comfortable and spend "regular" time. Some judges are finally recognizing that blocks of time are needed to parent a child. Hours of time are not enough. So make sure the judge gives you enough time with your children.

5

Alimony, Maintenance, and Child Support

Rule #71. Don't Expect Sympathy from the Court System—It Can Be Cruel out There

Alimony or maintenance are the payments you'll be required to make to your ex if you were the sole or primary breadwinner. Child support is payments you may have to make to your ex to help her with paying for expenses of raising the children. If you don't make your child support payments, even if there is a reasonable and valid explanation, the system may offer you little sympathy. How tough can it be? One of the Americans held hostage in Iran in the 1990s, Bobby Sherrill, was jailed the date after he returned home on charges of having failed to pay his child support. Another father, Clarence Brandley, was falsely imprisoned and served ten years in prison until exonerated. When released, he sued the state for wrongful imprisonment, wouldn't you? The state responded with a bill for $50,000 in past-due child support! How was he supposed to make payments while on death row?

No one can argue that a father who refuses to pay for the reasonable care of his children shouldn't be pressured to meet his responsibilities. However, the stories are in reality never as straightforward as the "bad dad" folks often say. The dad may have been totally and unreasonably shut out of his kids' lives. The dad may have suffered a debilitating illness, a loss of a job, or any of a number of reasonable constraints. The horror stories of how these dads are treated are far too numerous. The myth of the "bad dad" continues. So be prepared.

Rule #72. Get Real If You Want a Deal

What leads to anger in divorce is often the shock at what you have to shell out in alimony and child support. Many wives who bought into the myth (wife cooks and raises kids while husband brings home the bacon) expect to be very well compensated. You must look at your past lifestyle and expect to pay based on what it was.

"It's cheaper to keep her," says Lynne Gold-Bikin former chair ABA family law section and partner with Wolf, Block, Schorr & Solis-Cohen in Norristown, PA. You will never be happy with the results. The earlier you come to terms with it the better. Coming to terms with the fact that it's cheaper to keep her will give you the perspective you need to get through the divorce without making unnecessary battles you can't win.

It's easy to get angry in a divorce, but you're usually angry over what you have to pay your wife. If you're not surprised because you know what to expect, you won't get as angry, and if you're not angry you won't end up giving all your money to the lawyers while you fight to give your ex no more than she's entitled to. In many marriages, the men have or earn more money than their wives. As a wage earner, you may have made a deal with your wife that she would stay home with the kids and you would work. You may not like it, but you can't change the deal now! "Don't say you've been trying to get her to work for five years, you made the deal," says Lynne Gold-Bikin, Esq., of Norristown, Pennsylvania.

Rule #73. Know How Much and What Type of Alimony You Should Pay

There are several types of alimony, depending on your state's laws:

- *In solido*—This is a lump sum and is not modifiable; it is paid over time and cannot be increased or decreased.

- *Rehabilitative alimony*—With this type of alimony, the court determines the amount your ex needs for training to get into the job market. You may be able to later modify this award if your ex-wife doesn't use the money to rehabilitate and train herself. For example, your wife has a college degree and work experience before the children were born. If she could take a course and become certified to perform a well paying job but doesn't, the court may structure maintenance to encourage her to. If your wife develops a medical condition, she may be able to petition for more alimony. For example, medical problems may prevent her from obtaining the job she otherwise could have had.

- *Alimony in futuro*—This is alimony that continues until your ex-wife dies, remarries, or co-habits. For her to get an increase in the future, she must show material and substantial change in her circumstances, and the increase would have had to be unforeseeable at the time of the initial divorce decree. Your ex-wife will also have to show that her needs have increased. If she is an alimony candidate, it's better to negotiate a one-time payment and waive regular support payments to her (maintenance). "This is a missile aimed at your financial heart for years unless you defuse it," cautions Paul L. Feinstein, Esq., of Chicago, Illinois.

✔ *Reserved alimony*—In this arrangement, the court gives your ex-wife some payments for a period of time and reserves the jurisdiction so that your wife can come back later and request an adjustment. This may be mainly reserved for situations involving your wife's health, such as a debilitating disease. For example, if she's capable, of working now, but there's a possibility that her disease may recur, the courts might prefer the option of reconsidering. This approach is dangerous for you. The court may reserve alimony if your ex has been out of the workforce but has started an education to give her time to complete her education and see what she is capable of earning. As the husband paying alimony, you would prefer to pay for a finite number of years and then be free of any future payments. You want to avoid the second lawsuit when your wife can have the court reconsider her needs. Try to pay for it now. Pay her some sufficient amount of money and be done with it.

If you were married for many years and your wife cannot feasibly go back to work, try to settle for giving her a little more of the marital estate and a lump sum of alimony so there is more assurance that your ex-wife cannot come back for more alimony if she spends it all. Some courts have also used a hybrid approach that includes rehabilitative alimony and some smaller amount in futuro. The issues are fact driven, and the courts analyze all the facts involved. Consider the following scenarios:

✔ If yours is a 30-year marriage and your wife is in her late 50s and you're a successful CEO, the courts will clearly mandate that you pay alimony in futuro. To reduce this, you might try to agree to set up some type of annuity or argue that she's getting Social Security at some point, but that's about all you can do.

✔ If you develop a serious medical condition and are paying alimony in futuro at some amount, you can petition the court to reduce your payments to reflect the fact that you can no longer generate the same income because of your health problems. In such a case, therefore, you may not want a lump sum payout.

✔ If you voluntarily quit your business (e.g., if you sell your professional practice), the court may make you pay the same amount you've always paid, even though your own standard of living is now lower. So if you're going to sell, get two or three opinions as to the economic basis for the sale. You want to demonstrate that your selling is not just a vindictive ploy to reduce your alimony payments. Get a credible market analyst or business appraiser.

✔ Alimony is not always a foregone conclusion in some states, such as Illinois. If you give up substantial liquid funds and pay child support, the courts may reduce or eliminate alimony, says Paul L. Feinstein, Esq., Chicago Illinois.

"Maintenance has only been available in Texas for a short time, since 1997. Rehabilitative maintenance has been the common approach," explains Robert E. Holmes, Jr., Esq., of Holmes, Woods & Garza, in Dallas, Texas. For the ex-wife to receive maintenance, the couple must have had at least a 10-year marriage and your ex must need money to get rehabilitated. Alimony only applies in extraordinary cases. "We are the last state to have a maintenance statute adopted, but we remain a very favorable state for a man to get divorced." Women cannot tap into their husband's earning capacity.

✔ In some states, alimony may be terminated if your ex does not remarry but instead is cohabiting with another man in a manner similar to a marriage. A mere romantic, casual, or social relationship won't stop alimony. But if she's living with someone, it may enable you to have your alimony reconsidered. Check with your lawyer about the status of your state law.

✔ If you've realized a large capital gain, for example from the sale of stock options, this may not be income that you will realize in later years to support the payment of alimony and child support. So if there is any income on your tax return that is not going to continue in future years, document the support for your argument and give this information to your attorney. A one-time windfall should not be the basis of alimony in later years. The actual treatment will depend on the facts involved, the likelihood of recurrence, and your state's law.

Rule #74. Keep Records of All Your Alimony and Child Support Payments

You need to keep good records. Even if you hate paperwork, suffer through it. The IRS might challenge your alimony deductions. You'll need details and records to win the audit. Your ex may challenge you for not having met the requirements of the divorce or separation agreement. You can take several simple steps that will help you keep the records you need. Even if you can't keep them all, do as much as you can and strive to improve your documentation.* Here are some suggestions on how to get organized:

To get started, refer to the "bible" of your settlement, the final divorce decree. Make a copy of this and file it in a new loose-leaf binder behind a tab labeled "Agreement." Summarize the key payments you're required to make (and receive, if any). All the rest of your record-keeping decisions will be based on this data, as will your payments. This step is critical. If you don't know and understand all the details of your divorce obligations, you'll either overpay or underpay and have problems. Neither is a great option. Spend the time up front to analyze and summarize the key payments, noting any caps on the maximum you must spend and when they stop.

There are some great software products designed to organize personal finance. These include two of Intuit's products: Quicken (for personal finance) and QuickBooks (for closely held or small start-up business records) and general organizers such as Nolo Record Keeper, another excellent product. Using such software, however, does not replace the need to organize the paperwork related to your ongoing divorce responsibilities.

How can the fine computer software available help you organize all your original documentation in a consistent and manageable fashion? Consider the following suggestions. Use a computer check writing program to pay all bills. Before starting, set up new accounts that reflect the categories of information you may need to prove payments to the IRS or your ex. For example, add a category for alimony

---

*For additional information on budgets, organizing finances, and templates to use, see Shenkman, *The Beneficiary Workbook* (John Wiley & Sons, Inc., 1999).

if it's not included in the standard accounts that come with your software. Consider setting up sub or category accounts under the general caption "Alimony." Use the different categories of payments you're required to make to your ex under the divorce agreement. Similarly, set up an account called "Property Settlement—Paid" and "Property Settlement—Received" to track these payments or receipts.

Set up accounts for child support. If you have several children, you may wish to set up a "General" account as well as one for each of your children. You may also want to have a separate account for noncash payments. For example, if you have to pay tuition directly, set up a "Child Support—Tuition" account.

Use the computer check program for paying bills for all items. Voucher checks are the ideal way to organize personal and business payments to easily address billing problems, IRS audits, and other financial issues. For computer checks, you can obtain carbonless voucher copies of the checks as well. When you write any check, staple the voucher copy to the bill stubs that were paid. For example, if the divorce agreement requires you to pay 60 percent of all medical bills, attach a copy of the bill your ex gave you and show the calculation of the 60 percent on the bill. Then file these stubs in check number order in the binder you've set up, by year. The tab could be "2001—Check Vouchers."

If you ever give your wife cash (try not to), have her give you a receipt. Write a check out to yourself or cash and staple the receipt to it in order to keep all payments recorded in your computerized system.

These accounts should take only a few minutes to set up. Once set up, any time you need to check on payments, you can print a summary by account with the date, amount, payee, and comment column for every payment. This is a quick way to prove what you've paid. Consider setting up a separate account for "Child Support—Voluntary" and "Maintenance—Additional." If you make any type of indirect payments not required, track them. These could provide tremendous credibility to your attitude and efforts to help and be fair if your ex ever challenges your payment history. For example, if your wife calls and says that a child needs $250 for a school trip and your divorce agreement doesn't require you to pay this but you do anyway, categorize this in the "Child Support—Voluntary" account. This can show additional payments and help you have provided.

At the end of every year, print out a detailed run of all payments by account and save it in the loose-leaf binder you've set up, behind a tab with the year written on it.

If you can't or won't computerize your checkbook, use the same approach with paper copies. Buy "safety checks," which automatically produce a carbonless copy of every check as you fill in the actual check. Then file these with the attached receipts just as described earlier. In addition, you'll need to keep your own calculations since you won't have the computer's help. It's still simple (especially if you do it regularly). Buy a pad of 12+ column accounting paper (available in any office supply store). Set up the following columns across the top:

Date.

Check number.

Amount.

Payee (often your wife, but not always).

Comment/Description.

Record this information for every payment. Complete the following columns only if a particular payment belongs in that category:

Alimony—General.

Alimony—Medical.

Alimony—[any other categories contained in your agreement].

Alimony—Additional.

Child Support— General.

Child Support—Child A.

Child Support—Child B.

Child Support—Medical.

Child Support—Additional.

Thus, at the end of the year, the total of each column will give you the proof of the amount spent in that category for the year. The "Comment/Description" column is analogous to the "Memo" column available on many computerized check programs. Use this to indicate what the payment is for. If you're paying a particular tuition bill or medical bill, note the invoice number. If there is a question about the particular payment (e.g., you don't think you should really be paying it), note it in this column. You'll never remember the issues years later.

Save these accounting sheets in the binder you've set up as described.

Consider sending a photocopy of each year's computer report or accounting spreadsheet to your ex by certified mail, return receipt requested. You might wish to review this idea with your attorney. Then save a copy of everything you've sent your ex-wife, stapled to both the initial form and the certified receipt signed by her, in the same binder. This will prove that you've kept her fully informed. If she later claims you've shorted her on required payments, you have proof to demonstrate that you've made a good faith effort to apprise her of everything. This costs almost nothing to do and takes minimal time. The most important benefit might be that your ex may actually believe that you're being straight and trying to do your share. This could make the entire postdivorce relationship easier for all.

Rule #75. Demonstrate What Your Wife Can Earn

Get a vocational expert to come in to evaluate your wife's skills and abilities, to show she can go back to work and earn money, recommends Amy J. Amundsen, Esq., of Memphis, Tennessee. A positive benefit of this is that a good evaluation may help your wife gain insight into job opportunities that match her skills. Also, if your wife has taken care of your children but now the kids are in school and your wife isn't working, ask a psychologist to evaluate how much the kids still really need her services during the workday.

Rule #76. Help Your Wife Get Back on Her Feet

A frequent factor in determining the amount of child support and alimony that you will have to pay will be your ex-spouse's earnings. (Keep in mind that dividing your assets will help provide income and a base for your ex-wife to live from.) The sooner your wife returns to work and the more productive she is, the less of an economic burden the settlement will be on you. The disparity between various incomes is critical.

Basically, the courts are saying that if your ex-wife can eventually become reasonably self-sufficient, she should try to do so. If she's never worked and the best she can do is earn $10,000 per year, the courts won't make her do so, especially if yours was a long-term marriage. "The courts won't make your trophy wife go work at a burger joint!" states Paul L. Feinstein, Esq., of Chicago, Illinois. You can bring in a vocational expert to show what your wife is capable of earning. It depends on what she can legitimately and reasonably make.

Does this mean that you should stop supporting her? No. If possible, help her establish her own credit especially if she hasn't worked in a long time. This is not necessary if she is fully employed. She will probably have one or more credit cards, lines of credit, and so on. However, if she is a full-time Mom, she needs your support. Pay her bills, help out.

Let's say your ex doesn't work and hasn't for many years. Pay an employment agent, up front if necessary, to look for a part-time job (if the children are in school) or a full-time job (if the children are grown). Even if your wife doesn't show up for the interviews, you have the receipts. The judge may well consider your good intentions. It may even help your wife launch a new career, which will boost her confidence and earnings as well as minimize your alimony.

Provide psychiatric help for her if it will help her adjust to the new postdivorce circumstances. If you can minimize your wife's trauma from the divorce, it may make her less insecure, less antagonistic, and may increase the odds of her finding gainful employment. This is another reason using warlike tactics can be counterproductive.

Rule #77. Be as Methodical as Possible with Bank Deposits and Other Transactions

In analyzing your business and personal records, your wife's accountant may question every single deposit and check. The best approach is to be certain that every deposit ticket lists the check numbers, payers, and purpose of that deposit. Your checkbook register should do the same. If you are computer literate, put everything on a money management program so that you can easily list things in categories and fully disclose everything. Carefully describe each item in the memorandum or notation column the computer program provides for each check or deposit. If you don't do this on an ongoing basis, it becomes almost impossible after the fact to demonstrate what various transactions were for. Minimize the number of checks and large cash transactions since these will only draw questions to you. Use credit cards whenever possible to preserve a paper trail. The more details, the more forthright you will appear and the easier it will be to assemble data for the case. Remember that small acts of inappropriate behavior, such as unexplainable cash deposits, can create a pattern suggesting that possibly far greater financial misdeeds have been committed whether or not they actually have been.

Don't, however, dramatically change your spending habits in a short period prior to the divorce because significant changes will stand out.

If you're spending money on anything you shouldn't be, do the opposite of everything previously stated. Just expect to be raked over the coals if you're caught.

Rule #78. Keep in Mind That Your Standard of Living Establishes Maintenance Levels

The standard of living established during the marriage is what helps to set the target range for maintenance for your ex. Some husbands, out of guilt, encourage their soon-to-be ex-wives to spend, or they even spend on them! Guilt can do some amazing things. "One client of mine wanted to spend time with his honey, so he encouraged his wife to spend and travel," says Ginita Wall, an accountant and financial planner in San Diego. "The result was that he established a much higher standard of marital living that the court eventually held him to when setting alimony." The moral is: walk the middle path. Don't encourage a spending frenzy that will hurt you.

There is another take on this type of planning. Some wives may start spending sprees in anticipation of the divorce—buying jewelry, harassing you to buy them a new necklace, getting new furniture, or taking trips at times of the year during which you've never traveled before. And some husbands give in to this so their wives will stop pestering them. Is this the tactic their lawyer recommended? If this becomes the situation in your divorce, document how these expenditures were excessive by standards for the marriage, how they didn't occur in prior years, and how this pattern developed because your wife obviously was trying to boost her maintenance. The strategy could backfire to your benefit in that the court not only may recognize that these items shouldn't be included in the calculation of maintenance, but may even find she's wasted marital assets. This would certainly help your negotiation position.

Rule #79. Document All Cash Transactions

It's unavoidable to have cash transactions. These can include expenses paid in cash, cash withdrawals from the bank for spending, even some home repairs if the workers insist on being paid in cash. Document these to prevent your wife's attorney or forensic accountant from making inappropriate inferences. When you withdraw cash from the bank, keep some indication of what the cash expenditures are used for if you can. For example, note on the withdrawal slip what the withdrawal was for and save it with your monthly bank statement. This will avoid any adverse implications of large or ongoing cash withdrawals. Even if you have to estimate, it still will be far more credible than no information at all. Remember, a note that takes only 10 to 30 seconds each time you are standing in the cash machine line will never be able to be reconstructed with any amount of accounting assistance several years later.

Save receipts from cash expenses. Fill in a daily expense log to demonstrate your payments. This information will also help corroborate estimated living expenses listed on the case information sheet used in the divorce.

Rule #80. Don't Try to Starve or Freeze Your Wife Out

In ancient times a favored tactic of war was to create a siege of an opponent's city and deny them food, water, and other resources— in short, to starve or freeze them out. This tactic is not appropriate for your divorce. Don't let your anger or frustration get the better of you. If you've separated, ensure that your wife and children have adequate funds to pay for the mortgage, utilities, food, and other necessities. Refusing to pay these costs until the court resolves your financial dispute will only cause harm—to your family and you! If your wife wasn't looking for a war, you may push her into one. Your children will hate you for it (whether they are young enough to be living at home or not). It will reflect negatively on your character in court. So be a gentleman, it pays off in the end.

The more you intentionally leave your wife on financially reasonable footing, the less the court will take away from you. Don't go into the settlement process hoping to rake her over the coals. You are likely to get less than you might have otherwise achieved.

Although this advice is not the nasty, fire-spitting tone you want to hear if you're angry and neck-deep in divorce muck, it's the right advice for almost all situations. Nailing your wife to the wall just feeds the anger and animosity that the divorce process all too often fosters. No one wins—except maybe the professionals who bill hourly!

Rule #81. Analyze and Then Negotiate Responsibility for Your Children's Education Costs

Education planning is a key component in many settlements—it's a big number! "Be sure the divorce settlement makes it really clear whose obligation it is to pay for education and that assets are set aside for this purpose preferably in a trust," recommends Lori Sackler, Certified Financial Planner in New York City. Also make sure that the education fund is guaranteed, such as through insurance. Often the husband, as the primary wage earner, may be required to purchase life insurance under the agreement, but your ex may not be. "But if your ex is responsible for a significant portion of the education costs, she also should be required to obtain insurance. Otherwise, you could be holding the entire financial responsibility," cautions Sackler. Term insurance for the amounts involved can often be purchased at surprisingly low rates. Ask your attorney to include this requirement in the agreement.

If your settlement calls for a joint account to which you and your ex contribute quarterly (for example) to fund college costs, have your ex sign a letter approving the investment decisions. You don't want her coming back and suing you to pay more if the stock market tanks. This is analogous to what financial planners call an investment policy statement. You could use a similar form as a model, or just have her write a letter that you keep in the file.

Rule #82. Allocate Trust Funds for Your Children's Education and Other Expenses

If you have trusts set up for your children, make gifts of funds to them to assure a pool of assets for future college and other costs. This can ensure that you meet this important objective. It may help provide an older child with a bit more security through the uncertainty of the divorce process. It will protect the funds from the child's indiscretions and from creditors as well. This can also protect the funds from the court ordering a larger distribution to your wife and then saddling you with the additional responsibility of funding a substantial portion of the college costs from other resources.

Don't think you can get clever with trust funds, though, by pumping money in before the divorce and then taking it back after. The money in the trust is legally the trust's and not yours. You will trigger a host of tax and legal problems by taking the trust's money. Also, remember that you must disclose gifts in years prior to the divorce. If the court finds you were using this technique to hide marital assets, it may award your wife a bigger property settlement to adjust for half (or some other amount) of the "gifts." This result leaves you worse than having done nothing. Your kids may have $50,000 extra in trust, but your wife's $25,000 half will come out of your assets. The net result is you're cash poorer than had you done nothing.

Providing for the college education for the children after a divorce is a common problem. Your ex may be required under your divorce agreement to contribute to the future college costs. The problem this approach creates is that the agreement is merely a promise to pay at some future date. How do you get her to contribute her share years after the divorce is finalized, especially if she's angry? When feasible, a better approach is to use a funded education trust formed pursuant to the terms embodied in the divorce agreement. This avoids later fights to secure the promised payments. If structured with sufficient specificity and care, it can minimize or even avoid future arguments, such as how and when payments should be made, which educational expenses should be covered, and so on. If you set up such a trust, strive to include provisions in the divorce agreement that address the key terms to avoid a protracted negotiation when an estate planner later prepares the trust.

Consider the following issues and problems that may arise in negotiating this type of trust:

The generic specification of "college" or "post-high school" is common; however, your child may not pursue a college degree but instead might seek training in a technical school or in the arts. If this is not addressed in the terms of the trust, distributions from the trust may be prohibited.

What if there is an unforeseen medical emergency? Whereas the payment of medical expenses will always be dealt with elsewhere in the divorce agreement, the trust should permit invasion for emergency medical care, but only under very restricted circumstances (i.e., so as not to be used in lieu of either ex-spouse meeting his or her financial commitments).

Should the contributions you and your ex make to the trust be in cash, securities, or other property? If cash or property other than cash or marketable securities is contributed to the trust, complications of valuation may arise. Therefore, it is generally preferable to mandate contributions of solely marketable securities or cash. Tax basis issues may be relevant. Tax basis is generally what was paid for the property. The tax consequences of giving assets with low tax basis assets to the trust should be considered. The tax basis of the contributing spouse will carry forward as the trust's tax basis. For example, if your ex-wife contributes some dot com stock worth $50,000 to the trust for which she paid only $5,000, the trust will have to pay tax on the $45,000 gain if it sells the stock.

If feasible, it is preferable to have the trust completed before signing the divorce agreement and attached as an exhibit to the divorce agreement. This is rarely done, however, because it tends to complicate what is too often an already acrimonious or complex negotiation of the divorce agreement itself. However, you and your divorce attorney should weigh the desire of expediting settlement of the divorce itself against the risk that the trust to be negotiated later may become another round in the battle with your ex-wife.

Equal sharing of the legal fees may be appropriate to encourage your ex to cooperate and be involved. However, what if your ex creates substantial difficulties with knowledge that you must bear half the cost? Perhaps each spouse should bear half the cost of drafting the trust document and pay for any personal meeting time on their own.

The parents (i.e., you and your ex) are almost always named as co-trustees to manage the trust and make all decisions. This can be a substantial mistake because it forces you and your ex to continue to have yet another easily avoidable financial entanglement. Is it really appropriate for you and your ex to serve as co-trustees? It is far preferable to name a neutral, independent third party. If the funds involved are substantial enough, an institutional trustee (such as a bank) is ideal for such a situation. If the funds are not sufficient and the fees to use an institution would be excessive, then an independent party, perhaps a long-time mutual friend or accountant can be named. At minimum if you and your ex are named, then a third party or some mechanism to resolve disputes should be named.

If you and your ex are the sole trustees, far greater detail should be provided as to mechanisms for determining which expenses are acceptable, how and when they should be made, and so on to avoid later disputes. The best option is to retain an independent institutional fiduciary (trustee) who can carry out objectively the terms of the trust and make investment decisions appropriate to the circumstances.

Carefully consider the trust's decision making provisions. Should joint signatures be required on everything? Perhaps, specified expenditures agreed to in the trust—such as the payment of college tuition at an accredited university wherein the child is enrolled in a degree program—can be paid by any one ex-spouse acting alone. This will prevent one ex-spouse from stonewalling and using the trust funds as a tool to extract other concessions or results in the future. If different decisions require different approvals (e.g., anything other than tuition must be signed by both ex-spouses), the trust provisions must clearly delineate these requirements and care must be taken in completing the trust investment account applications to avoid inconsistencies.

The trust should grant both you and your spouse the right to name a successor if either of you can no longer serve. If your child is young, the trust could conceivably continue for more than 20 years. If individual successors are named, several alternates should also be specified. Too frequently, this vital issue is ignored.

If a named successor trustee is to act if a particular ex-spouse is disabled, a definition or mechanism for determining disability should be provided for. And if a successor is an accountant for the family or any somewhat more neutral party, definitions can avoid arguments as to when and if the successor can act or must cease to act. Also, provisions governing dispute resolution and decision making should be incorporated into the trust document to minimize potential future issues. However, the best approach, as noted, is to name an institutional fiduciary.

It is essential to provide for the distribution of funds remaining after the completion of college. These provisions should be drafted with sufficient flexibility so that the funds are used appropriately if the child does not attend college. What if the child only attends college after a delay to work? What about postgraduate studies? Apart from these obvious issues, it is advisable to specify whether the trustee should endeavor to assure that funds remain after college. Since the variations of the new uniform Prudent Investor Act (a law which governs how trust assets should be invested) have been passed in many states, a statement as to whether or not funds should remain after college payments, and to what extent and for what purpose, is essential to the trustee's determining the time horizon for investments.

From an income tax perspective, there can be an advantage of having some amount of investment assets taxed directly to the child. Even with the Kiddie Tax (which results in income of a child under age 14 being taxed generally at the highest-taxed parent's rate), a portion of income can be taxed at lower rates. Many parents will attempt to secure this benefit by retaining some funds in a custodial account (e.g., by using the Uniform

Gifts to Minors Act, "UGMA," or Uniform Transfers to Minors Act, "UTMA"). Trusts are taxed at the highest maximum rate once a modest level of income is earned. What can be done to reduce your taxes is to make distributions from the trust to the child's custodial account each year so that some portion of the taxable income is taxed at the child's lower tax rate. The problem with this approach is that over a number of years significant funds could accumulate in the hands of the child at too young an age. It also complicates the payment of college costs because the detailed distribution, investment, and decision-making provisions in the trust cannot be incorporated into a custodial account. Therefore, you must carefully weigh the minor tax benefits against the cost of dealing with future financial complications.

Rule #83. Find Out If You Can Get Alimony

Men assume that they must pay alimony to their ex-wives, but this is not always the case. A growing number of cases have allotted men alimony. As many as 5 to 10 percent of men qualify. The following factors, among others, may indicate that you are a possible candidate:

- ✔ If you moved from city to city to follow your wife's job relocations.

- ✔ If your wife is a highly paid executive.

- ✔ If you paid for your wife to go to college or graduate school.

✔ If your wife is in a high tax bracket and may prefer to give you alimony (which is tax deductible) than to transfer property to you.

✔ If your wife is independently wealthy.

Rule #84. Keep in Mind That Separate Assets Can Create Support Obligations

Any asset, even separate assets (e.g., assets you received as a gift or inheritance) may create support obligations to your ex and increase child support, depending on state law, notes Lynne Strober, Esq., of Mandelbaum, Salsburg, Gold, Lazris, Discenza & Steinberg in West Orange, New Jersey. Even if these assets cannot be directly added to a calculation, the court may still look at the income (including interest, dividends, and perhaps even capital gains) these assets throw off for determining your ability to pay support. In determining alimony, the courts will generally look at all your present income. Courts have even gone so far as to impose a reasonable interest rate on assets held by one spouse to determine support to pay another. If you've invested assets at a very low rate to reduce what you may have to pay to your ex, the court may impose a required return or assumed level of interest on these assets when making alimony and child support calculations. It is therefore becoming more problematic to insulate assets. If you have a trust and the trustee has the right to give you money at the trustee's discretion, it's unclear how the courts would view this arrangement.

Should you give up on insulating separate assets? Not at all. "Have your folks set up a trust for you under their wills or even while they are alive, for your life rather than giving you an outright bequest," recommends Lori Sackler, Certified Financial Planner in New York City.

The case that gave rise to this situation also points out one of the major problems with divorce law. The courts often face spouses who act unreasonably and reach conclusions to establish some degree of fairness or reasonableness. What can you do? Because the law is new, developing, and unclear, review these issues with the attorney handling your case. Some of these cases have reached to impute income because the husband involved was trying to freeze out his ex-wife and/or reduce child support. If you act reasonably, the conclusions of these cases may not be necessary or appropriate for your situation. The way the law often works in divorce is that the court won't expressly state that it used a broad or long-reaching approach because the husband in the particular case was a dirt-ball, even if that is obvious. Your ex-wife's attorney may try to take the conclusions of such a case and apply them unfairly to you even if you're not being a dirt-ball. This could be grossly unfair. Try to work with your lawyer to analyze the cases and distinguish the facts in your case to the facts from the cases that reached the unfavorable result. These cases, even unfavorable ones, may provide a road map for determining what you can and cannot achieve by planning steps.

The courts will look at income from all sources for child support and alimony purposes. But the courts may conclude that unless you received income from these assets on a regular basis they may not be considered as strongly, or even at all, according to Amy J. Amundsen, Memphis, Tennessee.

Rule #85. Limit Child Support When It Becomes Excessive

At some point if your income is too high, the child support you pay can become a windfall to your ex. "Once your income reaches a couple of hundred thousand per year or more, then the strict percentages state law may require for child support payments may not be appropriate . . ." says Paul L. Feinstein, Esq., Chicago, Illinois. Therefore, Feinstein recommends that if you're earning a six-figure salary, you should show your needs as well so that the courts won't blindly apply state guidelines and will avoid creating unjustified income for your ex-wife.

Don't get caught up in guilt and not address excessive alimony at the outset, because once it's set, you have to pay. If you miss or are late on even one payment, you risk problems with your ex-wife and possibly the court. The court awards alimony to provide your ex with a measure of independent living and requires you to pay it. If it's going to be unaffordable, address this before the agreement is concluded.

Rule #86. Don't Think That Moving Overseas Will Enable You to Avoid Paying

What if you want to move overseas to escape your alimony and child support payments? Although there are guidelines between states for enforcement of alimony, there are no international treaties. Some countries, especially European countries, have conventions (treaties or legal agreements with other countries) that are bilateral treaties. One country may have several conventions, but the rules in the convention are only valid and enforceable if both countries involved have agreed to the convention. Most countries don't. Therefore, if you are subject to a judgment in the United States for alimony and your wife seeks to enforce it overseas, she may find it difficult. Recognition of that U.S. judgment—and its enforcement in an overseas court in a country to which you've moved—may not be easy. Your ex would first have to take the U.S. judgment from state court and have it entered into the appropriate family court with jurisdiction in the foreign country and seek to have it approved as a local judgment there. Then she would have to seek to have that judgment enforced. So it's a two-step process. This can sometimes be difficult to accomplish. If you have a local attorney represent you, you may be able to argue against the entering of the judgment if no appropriate notice was given or if that judgment is against that country's public policy.

But before you hit www.cheaptickets.com for your one-way airfare, consider the whole picture. "If there is enough money at stake, and you haven't made yourself judgment proof, it will often pay for your ex to go after you. Many foreign countries have strong laws for liens. Some countries have strong laws for debtors' prison. If you have debts and don't pay, you can be imprisoned," says David Leitman, Esq., Herzilya, Israel. So before you leave, you had better do your homework.

There are also a host of different injunctions that your ex can obtain, such as a "Mareva injunction," which can be used to freeze your property overseas. If enough is at stake, your ex would probably go after these injunctions.

6

Negotiating the Property Settlement and Debt Allocation

Rule #87. Prepare Yourself Emotionally for the Potential Settlement

"Set your expectations to reality; if not, you're going to get [angry] when you find out what it's going to cost you," warns Lynne Gold-Bikin, Esq., of Norristown, Pennsylvania, who is also the former chair of the ABA Family Law Section and is on the Board of Governors of the American Academy of Matrimonial Lawyers. Expectations are extremely important. If you had an agreement with your wife that you would work and your wife would raise the kids, don't be surprised that you'll have to pay substantial amount. And keep in mind that your anger hurts no one but your children.

Don't compare what you contributed with what your ex-wife earned. It's often best to start with the mindset that everything is going to be divided 50/50. For a long-term marriage, even separate assets you owned before marriage may be commingled in the court's analysis, depending on the facts.

The 50/50 mentality is far different from the "I'll rake her over the coals" view too many men take. Going for that type of settlement is likely to increase legal fees, may anger the court, and could ultimately cost you a lot more. "You're almost always better off trying to negotiate from a position of reason than from a position of hardnosed unfair proposals," Gold-Bikin advises.

What this means is that although it might feel great to read those vicious antiwomen divorce books and articles when you're angry at your ex, her lawyer, and the divorce process, they won't do much to help you.

Rule #88. Pick a Negotiation Strategy

In planning your strategy to negotiate a property settlement, remember that you have an economic obligation to your wife and children. You will have to meet that obligation to some extent. So a strategy you formulate to avoid this not only will be ineffective, but will likely escalate the antagonism and the legal fees. It's really not worth paying $50,000 in legal fees to fight a $35,000 difference in the value of an asset. The legal system is a horribly inefficient and uneconomical battleground. Don't devise a strategy that causes you and your family as a whole to sacrifice more than you can gain.

Don't plan for what you might give up. "Fallback" planning puts you at a psychological disadvantage! It has a way of happening just because you thought of it. Make your list of demands and stick by them in the early stages of the negotiation process. Trade off with deliberation and caution. Focus on the one, two, or three key items you absolutely won't give up. Let the inevitable compromises take place naturally.

Some divorce strategists recommend including demands you know you won't get so that you can then give these up early and periodically as a means of saying "I'm being cooperative." It gets the process of trading off started and keeps it moving. On the other hand, making excessive, unreasonable, or obviously unattainable demands can set a tone of unreasonableness for the entire process. This can encourage your ex and her advisers to similarly make unreasonable demands. The two of you can rack up some impressive legal, accounting, and other fees while discarding goals that neither of you could reasonably have expected to achieve. Before pursuing a strategy of adding excessive demands to be able to give them up, make sure that it will really benefit you and the process. If the divorce negotiations can be handled by both you and your ex in a reasonable fashion, this approach would be counterproductive. If your ex is making unreasonable demands, perhaps you can first convince her and her advisers to be realistic. If not, you can counter with your similarly overreaching demands, but be prepared for a lot of unnecessary legal and other fees.

Leave the negotiating table when anger heats up. Cool down and return later. Angry people are losers.

It is not unusual for men to become adamant and to build walls they cannot get back over without embarrassment or heightened anger. Nevertheless, keep a lid on your emotions, stay loose, and make sure you say nothing you can't reverse to gain something that appears more important later on.

Negotiate from strength. The only way to do this is by being a realist. The driving force in a latter stage contested divorce is generally one of "screwing each other over." This doesn't work! Men who control their emotions do far better in settlement agreements than those who keep the hot poker roving. Whether you believe it at this stage or not, your spouse played a role in accumulating what you've got. Therefore, you're undoubtedly going to lose a meaningful portion of the marital assets, perhaps as much as 50 percent, sometimes less, sometimes more.

Expect to set your ex up so she can be as financially independent as reasonably possible. With this in mind you're free to concentrate on the *major assets* that you need to move on to the next phase of your life. The courts will ultimately seek to settle your dispute as win-win. When you're thinking win-win at the get-go, you put your opponent off-balance in negotiations. You have to give to keep what you have. Think hard about this last statement!

Don't get caught up thinking about the horror case your friend described or about the husband who got away with a sweet deal by stonewalling his ex-wife's accountant on valuation matters. These things happen, but they're not the objective, and they're not the typical outcome.

Rule #89. Determine Whether Your Divorce Is No Fault or Whose Fault

Many states have a no-fault divorce, which means that "being naughty" may not affect the financial aspects of the case. However, if your ex was pretty despicable, discuss the gruesome details with your attorney, and be sure your attorney is an experienced matrimonial litigator. It may be that even if your ex's actions are not legally included in the factors to be considered, they may influence the judge on subjective issues. The evidence might also be used carefully by your attorney to dissuade your ex from pursuing certain proceedings for fear of how the evidence could impact her case overall.

In one case, the husband booted up the wife's home computer while she was out and found numerous obscene e-mails to and from her lover. His wife then asked for money to obtain expensive cosmetic surgery under the care of a costly specialist in the Mid-west. From the e-mails, the husband knew this is where her lover had moved. He wished her bon voyage and discreetly hired a private eye who happened to be a good photographer, too. The costly surgery was actually far less costly, and the extra funds were used for fun in the sun with her lover. When the wife returned home, the husband filed for divorce and his lawyer was able to negotiate a quick and favorable settlement. The husband ultimately won a generous settlement of the bulk of the marital assets.

Rule #90. Use a Loan to Equalize Assets That Are Difficult to Divide

Sometimes it's tough to divide up assets even if you've worked out the amounts. Other than in the movie *The War of the Roses,* using a chainsaw to divide a house is probably not a typical approach. For example, if you or your ex have a professional practice together, you may not be able to transfer an interest in it (and even if you could neither of you would want this tie after the divorce). If there is enough cash, you can use it as an offset, but that's not often available. What can you do? "Consider using a promissory note to equalize the difference," suggests Ginita Wall, CPA, CFP, and author of *Smart Ways to Save Money during and after Divorce.* The note can be for the amount that is needed to equalize you or your ex for the hard-to-divide asset. The note should also provide for payments of principal and interest at some reasonable rate. The principal payments on the note should not trigger any tax consequences because it is incident to a divorce and the tax laws exempt such transactions from taxation. It might, however, be possible to still deduct the interest on the note, so check with your accountant.

Rule #91. Don't Nickel and Dime Just Because Your Ex Does

Getting worked up over small items is rarely worth the cost and problems it creates. Try to keep the big picture in mind, even if your ex doesn't. If your wife won't settle and either wants an unreasonable cash settlement or continues to nickel and dime you regarding items of lawn furniture or garden tools, for example, don't fall into the trap of trying to nickel and dime her, too. Her attorney (who knows that time is money) might also become exasperated with her and may be able to convince her to be reasonable.

In one situation, the husband agreed with his wife on an equitable split of all assets. Then, unexpectedly, she asked for an additional $45,000 cash settlement. This was the last straw for him. After all the detailed negotiations, during which he had calmly addressed his wife's nit-picking over low-value household items, the husband requested his attorney to call the wife's attorney, who also was at his wit's end, and ask if they might meet to review the status. The husband gave the attorney as much information as he could about the marital assets and the wife's feelings for certain assets. He also gave the attorney wide latitude to negotiate a final settlement, realizing that the continued nit-picking was running up legal bills and everyone's tempers. The husband's attorney mentioned to the wife's attorney that the husband was to receive as part of the settlement a fine oil painting worth $20,000 that his wife also coveted. A deal was struck. The wife agreed to take the painting in lieu of the cash request. The biggest benefit for all, however, was that the compromise ended the nit-picking that had threatened to go on forever.

Rule #92. Don't Let Your Insurance Coverage Lapse during the Divorce Process

It is critical to maintain your insurance coverage—for disability, life, casualty, and property—during a divorce process. Don't cancel important insurance coverage because of a cash flow crunch, especially one that may be only temporary. Speak with your life and disability insurance agent or financial planner. There may be ways to modify the policy to help you get through the financial pressures of the divorce without losing coverage. It would be tragic if death or disability were to occur after you had dropped coverage. Also, it would be a shame to drop coverage only to have to repurchase new coverage at more expensive rates in the future because you are older than when you originally took out the policies.

Property and casualty insurance is always essential. If the house burns down without coverage, everyone loses. Don't assume your wife is paying for premiums or maintaining coverage on family assets that she has. Find out. Make sure everything is covered. If cash is tight, contact your agents; it may be possible to reduce costs without letting coverage lapse (e.g., taking a bigger deductible, canceling pricey options). You may be able to stretch payments out to quarterly or even monthly instead of annually to help cash flow.

Some states, such as California, may issue temporary restraining orders to prevent you from dropping insurance coverage. "In one case the husband dropped his wife from his medical insurance coverage in violation of the court order," explains Ginita Wall, a San Diego accountant. "She became quite ill and ran up tremendous bills that were not covered. The court ordered the husband to pay all of the medical expenses out of his share of the matrimonial settlement,

119

with no offset or consideration to the impact these payments had on him. The judge was so furious with his brazen and inhumane actions that it tainted the entire settlement."

Rule #93. Understand Equitable Distribution

Most states use a concept called "equitable distribution" to divide marital assets. Although the rules differ in many important ways from state to state, there are some general concepts that may affect you. Understanding these concepts will help you settle quicker and often better. The premise of equitable distribution is that marriage is an economic partnership. Equitable distribution is intended to fairly distribute and allocate marital assets between you and your ex. Equitable distribution has spawned tremendous complexity, litigation, and problems. Implementing this simple and fair-sounding concept is anything but.

Although many ex-spouses may not feel that the property divisions were equitable, here's a list of some of the factors that many state laws direct the courts to consider:

- Length of marriage. The longer you're married, the more your ex is likely to be entitled to. If you just became a $50 million dot-com kinda guy, and you've been married for 30 years, including your entire working career, expect your wife to get a lot, maybe half.

- Monetary contribution to the marital assets.

- Tax consequences and characteristics of the various assets.

Rule #93. Understand Equitable Distribution

✔ Property ownership. Who owns what (i.e., "title" in legal jargon) doesn't matter. If you're a doctor and put all your assets in your wife's name to protect it from malpractice claimants, under equitable distribution you shouldn't suffer.

✔ Any asset acquired during the marriage. These are marital assets that are to be put into the marital pot to determine equitable distribution. The burden will generally be on you to show that any particular asset was a gift or inheritance (called "separate property") that should avoid the marital pot.

✔ Your business or professional practice. This asset is considered in determining equitable distribution. However, your license, degree, and professional skills or job may or may not be depending on state law.

✔ Each spouse's income and future income potential. If your wife has been a stay-at-home wife and you're a big shot, cigar-smoking executive, expect to pay more. She'll need it and the law provides for it.

✔ The value of property owned by each of you and marital property.

✔ Needs, responsibilities, and obligations of each spouse. You should be certain that these factors are properly disclosed and presented, because these factors could be critical to the settlement you ultimately receive. If one of you has special medical needs, or a condition affecting the ability to work, the court will consider this.

✔ Increases in the value of certain assets (such as a business) during the marriage. These are considered marital property. These rules can be complicated to apply and can differ in important ways from state to state. Be sure to carefully review them with your attorney.

- ✔ Liabilities and debts. Equitable distribution isn't only about assets. Liabilities and debts that must be considered include home mortgage, car loan, and so forth.

- ✔ Age, health, and other circumstances.

Rule #94. Be a Good Sleuth to Win the Divorce Lottery

Look for every indication of hidden assets or information. The more creative and clever you are, the better you will fare. One husband's astute eye won him the lottery. The wife had just won a $1.3 million California lottery! After 25 years of marriage, the lottery was (in her view) her ticket to a lot more than just financial freedom. She quickly filed for divorce. Well, maybe not that quick, she did wait 11 days after her December 28, 1996 winning before filing. The judge held that the wife had violated state law disclosure requirements and thus forfeited her entire interest in the lottery winnings to her now ex-husband. The court found that her actions were a fraud on her husband of 25 years.

The husband won the preceding case, big-time. But the sword can cut both ways. If you get caught lying on legally required disclosure documents, even if your ex doesn't end up with the whole pot, you could get really nailed. And you'll deserve it. There is a world of difference between negotiating for your best interests and intentionally deceiving your ex. Sure you've heard the stories of the "shrewd" husbands who have lied and won big. Some have. Many more have gotten caught, too. Is it worth the risk? The former lottery million-aire California wife probably doesn't think so!

Similar situations have arisen in many cases, although not as dramatic as the big lottery winning. For example, if your wife systematically hits the cash machine for $500 a week for many months before she files (when she hadn't used it much in the past), a fraud may arise. If she's been salting away the cash in a safe deposit box or separate bank account, and if she doesn't report the cash on the financial disclosure forms, it's fraud.

There are lots of ways for your ex to hide assets. Look for clues and unusual items like these:

✔ Larger cash withdrawals than customary.

✔ Cash withdrawals on credit cards that appear in your checkbook just like payments on the card.

✔ Bonuses, stock options or other deferred compensation. The smaller and more closely held the business, the greater the likelihood of this being hidden.

✔ Purchase of assets. If you think your wife is planning an exit (remember wives file first in the majority of cases), you might see a pattern of purchasing assets. For example, if your wife's car is a few years old, so that purchasing a new car wouldn't look unreasonable (even though neither of you would have otherwise purchased a car quite so soon), she might buy a new car. If your dining room furniture is rather old, your wife may suddenly buy an expensive new set even though she hasn't concerned herself for a decade with upgrading. She might all of a sudden push for a home remodeling that's been talked about for years. Why? Because a used car, dining room set, or home improvement may have little value when negotiating a property settlement, and may be assets that only she could use. This can provide her with some incremental financial leverage in the negotiations. However, if there's really a pattern of financial abuse, you might be able to shift the tables back against her.

✔ New accounts. Sudden appearance of new accounts in the names and Social Security numbers of your children may indicate advance planning.

✔ Inflated business expenses to reduce earnings. This can be travel expenses, larger than appropriate supply purchases, costly new equipment, salary payments or consulting fees to friends, and so forth.

✔ Deferral of income by failing to bill accounts in a closely held business or professional practice.

Rule #95. Assume Your Wife's Accountant Will Find the Bank Transactions You Forgot About

Frequently in a business or individual capacity, people apply for bank lines of credit and other matters where they are requested to disclose personal and financial data. Assume that any of these application forms will be discovered. Puffing to secure bank credit may be great if you get the line of credit but can be disastrous when your ex or soon-to-be-ex-wife's accountant discovers it during the investigation of your assets. If you've listed income or assets data on any applications or other forms (e.g., for a state or federal license or regulatory report), be certain that you discuss them with your attorney as early as possible in the case so you can deal appropriately with these matters.

If you know you were puffing (e.g., you listed on your mortgage application that your business was worth $1 million, when you know it couldn't be worth more than $400,000) 'fess up quick and explain the reasoning behind it. Being honest now can defuse a far worse problem later. The last thing you want is to have this type of issue come up while you're on the witness stand in the middle of a tough cross-examination.

Rule #96. Look for Bank and Other Transactions Your Wife "Forgot" About

Most books that describe a spouse hiding assets in a divorce tend to focus on the husband, but sometimes the guilty party is the wife. "Many wives clean out family bank accounts, spend the money, and then say they don't have it," notes Sidney Kess, CPA, JD, a New York City tax expert. "You have to carefully trace the funds from all the bank accounts. Don't overlook the fact that your wife may have a plan as well," he advises.

Kess relates the following case. The wife withdrew all the money from the family bank accounts and said she had nothing when the divorce later occurred. In papers her attorney filed with the court, she claimed her situation was so bad that she was about to go on welfare! Six months later, she married the kids' kindergarten teacher and bought a $150,000 house. "She had secreted the money to an unreported separate account," says Kess. So what can you do? "Look at all bank statements, get sworn affidavits that she has no other bank accounts, make sure all accounts reported on her income tax return have been accounted for. If you can get a mortgage or credit card application or credit card report, scan them for additional accounts. "If she later makes a large purchase, you can bring out the affidavits and challenge her," says Kess.

It's not only bank accounts you should search for carefully. "Check if she has another job on the side that you don't know about," Kess advises. How much is she earning? In most cases, the courts put all the burden on the husband. The wife may say she isn't working and the husband is viewed as the sole source of earnings. This assumption may not always be true, so check it out.

Rule #97. Protect Separate Assets from Your Ex

Assets that you received as gifts or inheritances are separate property that should not be reached by your ex as long as you retain the separate identity of these assets and do not transmute them into marital property. Keep any gift or inheritance separate. If the amounts are not that large, set up a special brokerage or bank account to hold solely these separate assets. If the amounts involved are large, consider setting up a revocable living trust as an accounting entity to keep property separate. However, if you have separate property and your ex-wife contributed to its appreciation (e.g., if she helped you pick the stocks or if she ran the computer program that helped you select the asset allocation) that appreciation becomes marital, warns Amy J. Amundsen, Esq., of Memphis, Tennessee.

If you have separate property, save the documents demonstrating that it was received by you as separate property. If you can, ask whoever gave you gifts to provide you with a copy of the checks. If the amounts were more substantial, obtain copies of the gift tax returns from your parents or whoever made the gifts. For inheritances, try to obtain a copy of the federal estate tax return that demonstrates what you received. If the estate was smaller than the amount required to file a federal estate tax return, obtain a copy of a state tax filing. Many states have inheritance or other taxes that are assessed at levels much lower than the federal estate tax. If these are not available, try to obtain a copy of the will and any releases signed when assets were distributed. These items can all help confirm the separate nature of the assets.

If your marriage was relatively short lived, some assets you owned before divorce may be held outside the settlement. Review this with your attorney because the laws differ from state to state and any decision will depend heavily on the facts involved.

Be careful how you handle separate assets. In one case, the husband used separate trust fund assets to directly pay for personal expenses, from vacations to a new sports car for the wife. Later, the husband transferred cash from his business to the trust to replace the monies previously spent. The marital expenses funded from the trust and the frequent commingling of marital assets (i.e., business earnings) with the separate property in the husband's trust resulted in the court finding that the trust assets had been so commingled, and the independence of the separate property so totally disregarded, that the entire trust was treated as a marital asset.

Rule #98. Recognize That Your Retirement Accounts Are Complex and Important

Ask the mediator and your attorney how they propose structuring the pension benefit to your ex recommends Saul M. Simon, CFP, financial adviser with Allmerica Investment Management Company, Inc., Edison, New Jersey. "Is it in your best interest to buy it out?" It may be advantageous to give your ex a lump sum in lieu of a periodic payment. But before you make any decisions, find out at what age you are eligible to receive this benefit, how much you are really entitled to, and how assured it is. "For many people, pension plans are almost a hidden or mysterious asset—they are complex and can abound with tax and other problems, legal restrictions, and formalities," cautions Simon.

You have to be extremely careful—and often patient—in planning for retirement accounts. Sidney Kess, a noted New York City attorney and tax accountant, tells of a case where an impatient, penny-wise and pound-foolish husband lost out big time. The husband was anxious to get out of the marriage. The wife was not earning much but had participated in a TIAA-CREF pension plan when she was teaching before their child was born. The husband went to a storefront lawyer for a quick and cheap divorce. Cheap is exactly what he got. The attorney never did the due diligence he should have. The pension was never discovered. And it wasn't a trifling amount either. It had grown through years of the bull stock market. The husband ended up losing out on the main asset of his wife, which he should have had an interest in.

The moral of this disaster is simple. "Many average people going through divorce go to general practitioner attorneys, or to the lawyer that appears to be the least expensive," observes Kess. "You just can't afford to take the risk [so] get an expert."

In another case, a husband went to a general practice lawyer. The wife had cleaned out all the bank accounts. The husband, who worked as a city employee, had no identifiable assets. However, under the retirement plan with his city employer, once he reached age 50, he would have certain options. In drafting the clause in the divorce agreement as to how pension assets would be divided up, his attorney didn't evaluate all the details of the plan. "Many plans include options that permit you to take different annuities as different requirements are met. For example, if you work 20 years and stop at 50 or older, you might get half your salary," notes Kess. In this particular case, the husband's general practice attorney was obviously not experienced with pension plans. He didn't even call in an outside expert. The result was that the divorce agreement was drafted very poorly. "It wasn't clear," comments Kess, "whether the husband could select to take a pension for his life which would end on his death, or whether he would have to take a joint-and-survivor annuity, which would mean that on his death his ex-wife would then receive payments. When the pension came due, the wife argued that it should be a joint-and-survivor annuity so it would continue after he died. Since this wasn't spelled out, they had to go back to court," explains Kess. "The cost of a second court proceeding was far more than it would have cost to have hired a specialist in the first place to do the job right! Many general practice attorneys, and even some matrimonial specialists, aren't familiar with pension and QDROs, so be careful!" warns Kess.

Rule #99. Protect Your Pension Retirement Assets

Retirement assets can be settled by an offset of other assets. For example, suppose you have a $50,000 IRA or retirement plan and a $40,000 bank account. Maybe your ex will agree to take the bank account as an exchange for your keeping the IRA account because the bank account won't trigger income tax when spent, but your withdrawals from the IRA or retirement plan will. She may view the differential as a reasonable allowance for tax costs (you may not). For example, if you're in a 30 percent tax bracket, withdrawing the IRA of $50,000 could trigger a $15,000 tax so you only net $35,000. This is $5,000 less than your ex got with the bank account. If you're under 59½ you could face a penalty too! Another alternative is to split the retirement plan between you and your ex by use of a qualified domestic relations order ("QDRO"). If your ex has a retirement plan for which you're negotiating a QDRO, carefully determine whether she has any loans outstanding, how they will be handled, and the impact on your settlement.

For example, assume that you have a vested pension worth $600,000 and the agreement provides that your ex-wife is entitled to one-third of the total. The easiest way to deal with this is for you to pay your ex-wife $200,000 out of other assets and collect the pension at retirement. However, this may not be a practical way to split up the pension assets because of the current cash drain you incur. This is where a QDRO can help. A QDRO is a court order dividing retirement benefits between the participant and an alternate payee. The alternate payee must be either a spouse, a former spouse, a child, or some other dependent. The majority of the time the alternate payee is a spouse or former spouse. In the preceding example, you can give your ex-wife one-third of your current retirement benefit as part of the divorce settlement and not have any current cash outlay. Your ex-wife would receive a portion of the retirement benefits under the terms of the plan. A QDRO is the only way to secure direct payment from the retirement plan in the case of a deferred division of retirement assets.

A QDRO must stipulate the following four items to be binding:

1. The name and the last known mailing address of the participant and the name and address of the alternate payee (in this case and throughout the following description, this is your ex-wife).

2. The amount or percentage of the participant's benefit to be paid by the plans to your ex-wife or the manner in which the amount or percentage is to be determined (e.g., 25% of the monthly benefit when payments commence).

3. The number of payments or periods to which the order applies.

4. Each specific plan to which the QDRO will apply. A participant in both a pension and profit-sharing plan can have the QDRO effective for only the pension plan, or vice versa.

What the QDRO must establish is the parties involved (you and your ex-wife), the specific plan(s) and definable or precise amounts of benefits relinquished by you to your ex-wife.

The QDRO is legally binding to the plan administrator to which the order applies and gives your ex-wife most of the same rights as other plan participants. The order cannot require the plan to provide increased benefits or pay benefits that are already spoken for from a previous QDRO. A QDRO is exempt from the anti-assignment rules.

When the QDRO applies to a defined benefit plan, distributions to your ex-wife can be made only according to the plan provisions, except for the earliest retirement age provision, as described here. Your ex-wife cannot receive more benefits than you would be eligible for at the time of payment. The distribution starting date is the earliest retirement age. This date is determined by the earliest date benefits are payable to the beneficiary or the later of the date benefits would begin if separation of service occurred or when you reach age 50. This precludes you from delaying your retirement to postpone payments to your ex-wife. This is an important exception to the rule that the order may not require the plan to provide any benefit or option not otherwise provided by the plan.

In some instances, a divorce settlement places a present value of the retirement benefits and allows the participant to retain these benefits but compensates the spouse in some other fashion. This does not qualify as a QDRO because there is no provision for an alternate payee. The amount of benefit to be received by your ex-wife is determined by the plan formula assuming you ended your employment with that company on the day payments are to commence. For example, suppose your ex-wife is to receive one-third of the total benefit and she elects to receive a monthly pension benefit commencing when you reach age 55. At age 55, the monthly benefit is $450, so she will receive $150 per month. If you actually retire at age 62 and receive a $600 monthly benefit, then your ex-wife would not receive one-third of the new total, but only the original amount, $150 each month. You ex-wife may elect any distribution method that the plan provisions allow. The distribution method chosen by your ex-wife has no consequences to you and your benefits.

Defined contribution plans are not as clear-cut. This is due, in part, to the future retirement benefit being unknown at the time of the divorce arrangements being determined. Generally, a QDRO may be used to reach a participant's account only to the extent the account is available for immediate withdrawal by the employee. Therefore, employer contributions that are in your account cannot be allocated under the order, even if vested, if the plan only allows for the amounts to be withdrawn on death, disability, or your termination of employment. Allowing the QDRO to attach, and force, withdrawal of employer contributions would provide increased benefits (immediate withdrawal of employer contributions). A QDRO is not permitted to increase benefits.

A QDRO's applicability to a 401(k) plan is based on the plan provisions. To avoid all current taxation, all employee contributions are construed by the IRS to be employer contributions. Consequently, your entire account balance is deemed to be from employer contributions and leads to the problems mentioned previously. An exception to this rule exists if the present value of your ex-wife's benefit does not exceed $3,500 or if your ex-wife consents in writing to such a distribution. Normally, the plan will allow early distributions if the tax laws permit them without disqualifying the plan.

The tax implications depend on the circumstances. Payments made to your ex-wife as the alternate payee are taxable to her, and not to you as the plan participant, unless the payments are for child support obligations. Otherwise the payments are taxable to you. Since the payments are received directly by her from the plan, the benefits are not considered alimony. If the plan was contributory, the basis in the contributions is to be prorated between you and your ex-wife. Your ex may also roll over a lump sum distribution into her IRA account and defer the tax. Regarding you as the participant, distributions made pursuant to a QDRO will not have any effect on your future eligibility for favorable tax treatment. For a better understanding of how to protect your pension assets, talk to your accountant.

Rule #100. Know the Laws If You Live in a Community Property State

"Community property" is a special set of rules governing how assets are to be owned. These rules apply in the states of Arkansas, California, Idaho, Louisiana, Nevada, New Mexico, Texas, Washington, and Wisconsin.

"The concept of community property is that whatever the fruits of the marriage are, we are going to divide that equitably (not equally) between the parties," explains Robert E. Holmes, Jr., Esq., of Holmes, Woods & Garza, in Dallas, Texas. When you enter into divorce, all assets are presumed to be community property in Texas except assets that were acquired prior to your marriage, or that were acquired by gift or inheritance. If you inherit assets that generate income, the income earned is community property. But the growth (e.g., stock market increases) remains separate. So if you were given stock valued at $100 and it is worth $10,000, the $10,000 worth of stock is still separate property. But the cash dividend earned is community property. The rules are pretty rigid in application.

In Texas, the law states that the person with lower income and lower capacity to earn may receive from the court more than half of the couple's community property assets. But if your ex gets 60 percent of a small estate, it really won't help her much if she isn't getting maintenance payments, so the theory doesn't work well in many cases. Most cases stay 50/50 or 60/40 at most. The women could be in a bad spot as a result of this type of settlement. A woman may have no earning capacity and her husband could divorce her with little obligation to support her, even if there are only modest marital assets. Contrast with other non-community property states where you're ex may get a smaller property settlement but large annual alimony payments.

Before hitching up that U-Haul to move to Texas, consider this. If you and your not-quite-ex move to Texas, you must live there for six months for Texas courts to have jurisdiction (i.e., the right to decide your case). If you move alone, it might be pretty hard to get Texas law to apply. "I wouldn't bank on it if your wife doesn't move to Texas with you," says Holmes. But if you can make it work, and if you're the one with the money, Texas is the place to be.

"There are some angles to try to take advantage of," notes Holmes. For example, if your ex's estate is large, you may make a claim for "equitable reimbursement" to the community property estate if she's used community property to reduce debt on a property she owned and ask for reimbursement or relief from the court. If the wife took $50,000 of community property cash and paid off a loan on a mansion she owns, you're entitled to an adjustment.

Rule #101. Keep in Mind That Debts May Present Community Property Issues

Debts are included in the determination of the value of net community property assets. However, if the debt was incurred by your wife on separate property, the debt should not be reflected in the determination of community property assets.

Rule #102. Settle Your Case If It Is Highly Technical and Complex

Perhaps as many as 90 percent of matrimonial cases end up settled and never see a courtroom. It's always better to settle unless your ex-wife is being impossible. There is a lot of uncertainty with one person—the judge—making all the decisions. Just because you and your attorney understand the highly technical points of an analysis (e.g., concerning the valuation of a high-tech business you own a percentage of) doesn't mean the judge has the technical background to understand it. Even if the judge has the ability, the adversarial proceeding can often obscure an already complex issue. When this is coupled with the tremendous pressure that many judges experience because of a heavy caseload, you cannot assure that the judge will understand the essential points to settle your case fairly. "This is why if there are highly technical issues you're better off settling," suggests Paul L. Feinstein, Esq., Chicago, Illinois.

Rule #103. Don't Underestimate the Judge

Don't misunderstand the comments in the prior tip. Although many judges may be overworked and some may lack technical expertise or have factors obscured in the rancor of a heated trial, don't underestimate your judge. If you attempt to deceive the judge, this will color every other issue in the trial.

For example, if you have a closely held business and have an insurance buyout agreement for $1 million for your one-half interest, don't reduce the insurance coverage to a mere $200,000 the month or even the year before the divorce to imply a lower value. Courts have enough familiarity with most of the games you are likely to play in your business that you will end up doing yourself more harm than good. Judges know lots of stuff. They know how you can cut a deal with a partner to lower the certificate of stated value on your interest in a closely held business, how you can use deferred compensation arrangements in lieu of a higher current salary, how you may be hiding travel and entertainment expenses, and all sorts of other tricks. Most judges weren't born yesterday, and you are unlikely to be the first husband to try to conceal assets. So think through the consequences of your action. Don't be swayed by the story of the husband who hid inventory in a closely held business and shorted his wife. Most of these stories are just like stock market investing. Do you know anyone that hasn't beaten the market? You only hear the stories about those who beat the market even though it's obviously impossible for everyone to be a winner. It's just as unlikely for most husbands to sham the court. It just isn't the norm. So don't try it.

Rule #104. Keep Alert for Steps Your Ex Might Take Affecting Assets

Eyes Wide Shut may be a catchy movie title, but it's not the way for you to act when a divorce is brewing and stewing. Do *not* get caught unaware. You do not want to be blind-sided. If you're not paying attention, your wife might take steps, whether out of anger or some plan that could be detrimental to you. Don't assume that just because a particular action is also detrimental to her she won't pursue it. If her emotions are charged and her anger heated, she may hurt the entire family, just to exact some pain from you. She might clean out your joint bank account and max out your joint credit cards. She may get a court order kicking you out of the house. She may freeze your 401(k) account with a court order.

For example, one husband was recently in the midst of an ugly divorce. His wife had maxed out his credit cards to the limit of $60,000. When his lawyer brought this up in court, she stated simply that she had purchased some clothes. The judge yawned. Whether right or wrong, justified or not, the husband lost out big time! The moral is keep your eye on your finances to catch something as quickly as possible. Ask your attorney what protective steps you can or should consider taking as early in the process as possible. But don't take this advice too far; if you start posturing, and your wife had intended to be reasonable, your actions might just be the catalyst of the very firestorm you were hoping to protect yourself against.

Along similar lines, another man discovered during his divorce proceedings that his wife had taken $200,000 out of various joint accounts and gave the money to a local church. The judge did *not* deduct the $200,000 from her share of the final settlement. Why this result occurred could have to do with myriad other reasons, but the bottom line again is that failing to pay attention was a costly mistake.

Rule #105. Protect Your Stock Options and Other Contingent Assets

Under current law in Tennessee, unvested stock options are not considered marital property. They are considered too speculative and may require continued employment after the divorce; and because the stock price may decline, they may not even be an asset.

There is only one case that said unvested stock options are not marital property, but this may change in the future, cautions Amy J. Amundsen of Memphis, Tennessee.

The moral is that when you're negotiating a property settlement, be careful to review with a matrimonial attorney the legal status and nature of any unusual or risky assets. If you have assets that may appear typical (e.g., an interest in a closely held business or a 50 percent interest in a rental apartment) but there are unusual circumstances, be sure to inform your attorney. These circumstances could substantially change the value of these assets for distribution purposes. For example, the closely held business interest may be subject to a lender's strict financing arrangement with loan covenants that may have been violated. If a loan could be called at any time this could affect the value of the asset. Or the rental real estate may be owned with a cousin who has control through the provisions of a partnership agreement. If your cousin, and not you, makes distribution decisions you may not have much control over when you get money. Think carefully through all the details of each asset to identify any points that have to be considered.

Rule #106. Remember That Settlements Are Not Only about Cash

Think in broad terms. A property settlement isn't only cash and the house. Consider accepting furniture in lieu of cash. It might make for an easier trade-off. You'll need furniture to set up your new residence. If you spend cash to get it, so consider taking furniture from the marital home. Keep in mind that household effects are very expensive. Although your soon-to-be-ex may concentrate on cash, you might do well to concentrate on trading for assets. Your spouse may think "cash-in-the-bank" so she can pay future bills and have security. This may enable you to get past a deadlock. It may also enable you to give your spouse more of what she wants and save yourself money by getting assets that would cost you more to replace.

Rule #107. Get All the Details Clear and in Writing

Generalities won't help. Determine who should be responsible for each debt of the marriage. Creditors won't necessarily recognize the allocation of debts in a divorce agreement. They just want to be paid, and they don't care who pays. Be sure that the separation or divorce agreement you sign is specific about who pays each creditor, how much, and when. If not, creditors you thought were your wife's responsibility may still be knocking on your door (and showing up on your credit report).

Rule #108. Find Out about Your Ex-Wife's Debts and Liabilities

Property settlements are not only about dividing up assets; debts must also be considered. Your property settlement negotiations present traps for joint debts, which you must be careful to address. Debt management is vital. When husbands and wives borrow, they generally do so jointly. Most assume if they owe a credit card company $10,000, they can each pay their respective $5,000 share and be all set. Not true. These debts almost always hold you and your ex jointly and severally liable.

In the typical matrimonial settlement scenario, one of the spouses—often the husband—assumes responsibility for the joint obligations. You would then pay these in lieu of some portion of the maintenance you would otherwise pay your ex. Alternatively, you may use your agreement to pay off certain debts as an offset to enable you to keep a particular asset. Thus, you are taking responsibility for what is technically a joint obligation of both you and your ex.

What happens if your ex-wife, who promised to pay a particular credit card bill of $10,000, remarries and has no money to pay it? The credit card company will contact *you* to pay because your wife can't pay. You may still be liable even though your wife had expressly agreed in the divorce agreement and assumed responsibility to pay that debt. Next, suppose your ex files for bankruptcy because she cannot pay and she lists the credit card company under her listing of creditors as required under law. In this scenario, your wife would typically file for a Chapter 7 bankruptcy, and she would be discharged from the obligations listed, including the $10,000 credit card debt. Your ex no longer legally owes the credit card company anything and they can't come after her. But they can sue *you* and get a judgment. Because of the terms of the divorce agreement, you may think you're not responsible, unfortunately, you are. So you may feel even more bitter and cheated.

So what can you do? There is a provision in the Bankruptcy Code that could ensure that your ex remains liable by having that credit card debt excepted from discharge in her bankruptcy. This way, her obligation will remain live after the bankruptcy. Any debts that your ex agreed to pay in the written separation agreement can be excepted from bankruptcy discharge. On the other hand, if your ex files for divorce *before* a written agreement is completed, there is nothing you can do. Therefore, you may want to push your ex to sign the agreement before she can declare bankruptcy to avoid this scenario.

Another approach is to require your ex-wife to reallocate debt between the two of you. For example, have your wife take out a loan or some other cash advance and pay off the joint debts for which she is liable. If you are not a signer on this new debt, then you should be safe. This type of planning should be permitted under the Bankruptcy Code.

If you and your ex-wife signed a separation agreement and your ex subsequently files for Chapter 7 bankruptcy, you could bring an "adversary proceeding" in the bankruptcy court to get a judgment to except particular debts from discharge. The bankruptcy court must go through a complex balancing test to determine who is more able to afford to pay off the debt. This could include an analysis as to whom the court believes it would be the greatest burden to pay the debt; you or your ex. This proceeding must be brought within 60 days of the first meeting of creditors in the case. All creditors get notice, if your wife files for bankruptcy, and her attorney will list you because your wife wants to discharge any obligations she has due to you. Your ex-wife's promise to hold you harmless on certain debts is an obligation, so you must be listed in her bankruptcy proceeding if she is to get relief from what she owes you.

If you and your ex-wife do not have a written separation agreement, the preceding planning won't work. What can you do? If all your assets and debts are held jointly, and if your ex-wife files for bankruptcy, there is no basis for your ex-wife to discharge anything. There is no way to take advantage of this provision in the Bankruptcy Code. You have no remedies. Your only option is to file for bankruptcy yourself. This happens too frequently. Many times there is no alternative because there is not enough money to pay off the debts. Often, this happens for good reasons—catastrophic medical expense, loss of job, or the high cost of maintaining two homes. In these situations, bankruptcy is a good-faith, last-resort remedy.

Another option may be to allocate debt in a way that it will get paid, says Colleen A. Brown, Esq., U.S. Bankruptcy Judge for the District of Vermont.

Rule #109. Don't Sign a Bad Deal Intending to Break It Later

"Don't sign a divorce or separation agreement to pay debts with the intent to file bankruptcy later to discharge those promises. The judge may find you guilty of fraud and you won't get out," cautions Colleen Brown.

Rule #110. Beware of Refinancing the House

If your marriage isn't going well, the red light should go on if your wife asks you to refinance the house.

For example, consider this scenario. A wife who owned a child-care facility recently coerced her husband into refinancing the house. She used the funds to pay off her car loan and credit card debts, and to purchase expensive computer equipment for her business. One night, she also provoked a fight with her husband when he returned home after having enjoyed several cocktails with friends. After pushing all of her husband's hot buttons, she called the police and her husband went to jail. When he was released and returned home, all the computer equipment was gone, and his wife had moved out into an apartment. The moral is that if divorce looms on the horizon be very cautious about any significant financial transaction. A new loan may just end up as a burden for you.

Here's another example. Several years ago a man went through a messy divorce. The house was in both names and had a low 5¼ percent mortgage. For financial reasons, he suggested they keep the house in both names and that off the books he would give her a quit-claim deed (legally giving her sole ownership by transferring any rights he had in the house to her) in exchange for a promissory note providing him with a percentage of the profits when the house was sold. She refused and said she wanted the house on the books solely in her name. He argued that this meant a new mortgage for her including closing costs. She wouldn't listen. She then nagged him until he agreed to have the deed recorded in her name only and paid off the mortgage. The new mortgage cost her 7¼ percent, plus closing costs. The additional monthly payments were $350. She reflected this new higher monthly cost on the court-required expense-reporting forms. This higher expense then became the basis for a higher monthly child support and maintenance from the husband—not a winning proposition for him.

7

Dealing with a Business or Professional Practice

Rule #111. Use a Voting Trust to Protect Your Business while Settling Your Divorce

A voting trust is a legal arrangement in the form of a trust, where shareholders have their stock voted by a designated person who is the trustee of the voting trust. A voting trust agreement provides the trustee an irrevocable right to vote stock in a corporation for a designated period of time (ten years being common). The trust does not grant the trustee the right to sell the stock or receive the dividends paid on the stock. Depending on state law, it may even be illegal for the trust to provide for these rights.

A voting trust can be an effective tool for structuring a matrimonial settlement where a significant marital asset is stock in a closely held business. You, as the spouse who is active in the business, and other shareholders, will generally insist that your ex-wife, as the nonactive spouse, not become actively involved in business matters, and in particular, not have any right to vote. Voting trusts are an excellent method to permit you to continue to control the business, while also allowing your ex-wife to protect her interest during the divorce settlement agreement by continuing to own stock in the business.

Suppose you own 60 percent of a design business. Your ex-wife is awarded 25 percent of the value of the business as part of the equitable distribution divorce settlement negotiations. You have resigned yourself to transfer to your ex the amount necessary to resolve the divorce; however, if you actually transferred 25 percent of the stock to your ex you would lose control of the business (because you would control only 35%). Worse yet, you would have put a sizable portion of the stock into the hands of someone who may be averse to the business and other shareholders. If there are insufficient other assets available for the distribution, you may have no choice. The solution could be to give your ex the 25 percent of the stock but require the transfer of her shares to a voting trust controlled by you. (To fully protect her interests, however, your ex should also negotiate an agreement that has reasonable restrictions on how much you and other shareholders can withdraw as salary or benefits. Without this additional protection, there may be no money left in the corporation for distribution as dividends on the stock.)

In one case, a court refused to permit an ex-spouse to revoke a voting trust agreement. The court reasoned that because the use of the voting trust arrangement for a closely held business was bargained for at arm's length and was an integral part of the divorce settlement agreement, the ex-spouse should not be able to change it.

Where a voting trust is going to be used, five steps are necessary:

STEP 1. The shareholders who will participate in the voting trust arrangement must draft a voting trust agreement.

STEP 2. The corporation must approve the voting trust agreement. This could require an action of the shareholders or board of directors, depending on the terms in the corporation's bylaws or certificate. Consent of all the shareholders may have to be obtained to comply with an existing shareholders' agreement. Some courts have held that a voting trust agreement is not valid unless a copy is filed with the corporation.

STEP 3. When both spouses agree on the terms of the voting trust agreement and a trustee is selected, the agreement should be signed by each shareholder who will participate, the trustee, and the corporation (an officer, often the president, signs in his official capacity on behalf of the corporation). Consideration should be given to having the successor trustees execute the voting trust agreement at inception, agreeing to be bound by its terms. The corporate minutes described in Step 2 are a prerequisite to an officer of the corporation being able to sign the trust.

STEP 4. Each shareholder who has joined in the voting trust arrangement then transfers his or her stock certificates to the corporation, which then transfers the stock to the trustee of the voting trust. In the above example, this would be your ex transferring 25 percent of the stock. If the stock certificates are merely handed to the trustee and not transferred officially on the corporation's books, the shareholders may not be prevented from voting their shares of stock. Each spouse's rights as a holder of a voting trust certificate is governed by the provisions of the voting trust agreement and any applicable local laws.

STEP 5. The trustee issues voting trust certificates to each shareholder. These could be held in escrow pending performance of other aspects of the divorce settlement.

The agreement can be quite simple and straightforward. It should indicate the name of the trustee and the shareholders who are participating. Be certain to review applicable state law and the corporation's shareholders' agreement, bylaws, and certificate for any additional requirements or restrictions that could affect the voting trust agreement. The length of time for which the voting trust will last should be specified. This should not exceed the shorter of any state law limitation on the period for which a voting trust may last, or the period for which the payments (e.g. dividends) will be paid to the nonactive spouse. The fact that all income will be distributed by the corporation directly to the shareholders, and not retained by the trustee, should be stated in the agreement.

The responsibilities, duties, powers, and rights of the trustee must be specified in the trust agreement. These specifications obviously have to reflect the terms of the divorce settlement, and the restrictions on the nonactive shareholder. Since the nonactive spouse (i.e., your ex-wife) is probably to be prohibited from changing or revoking the voting trust agreement, the documents should state this. If the trustee is to be compensated, the exact arrangements should be spelled out in the agreement. This will depend in significant part on whether a neutral person who is not involved with the business will be serving as trustee.

The agreement should clarify the rights of the nonactive spouse receiving stock held in the voting trust. For example, the following provisions are common:

> Each shareholder shall be entitled to receive, and shall receive, payments from the Trustee of all cash dividends or other distributions made by the Corporation with respect to the stock of the Corporation held by the Trustee hereunder. Any and all tax benefits each Shareholder shall recognize shall be the same benefits which would be recognized had that Shareholder held said Shares directly.

Rule #112. Gather the Information Necessary to Value Your Ex-Wife's Business or Professional Practice

If your wife has a business or professional practice, you should have it appraised before negotiating the property settlement. Similarly, if you have a business or professional practice, your ex is going to want to get a valuation of it so she can protect herself in the settlement negotiations. Even your lawyer wants full disclosure to the appraiser—he won't want to be sued later for not protecting you (or your wife in the case of her attorney). So whichever side you're on, save potentially huge avoidable professional fees by putting together the key basic data every accountant, appraiser, or attorney will need on a closely held business or professional practice. The following lists will help you evaluate your wife's business or practice.

First, evaluate the nature of your practice or business. If you wife is a partner (either a shareholder or a member) in a large practice, the partnership agreement should be evaluated; this applies to both shareholders and operating agreements. If the partnership has other partners, reasonable buyout provisions, and so forth, it will be an important factor in the analysis. The analysis of professional firm partnership agreements has been described in many cases, articles, and other authorities, so review the implications with your attorney. A more difficult situation is where no partnership agreement exists, which is typically the case in a smaller firm or for a sole practitioner. In these instances, the only source of information may be a subjective evaluation of the practice or business by an appraiser and application of industry standards.

Second, you need to perform due diligence and data gathering. There are five key areas to consider:

1. *General document request checklist:*
    - ✔ Financial statements for the past five years. Sometimes three or four may be accepted.
    - ✔ Tax returns for the past five years. Sometimes three or four may be accepted.

- ✔ Articles of incorporation of the business or the comparable legal documents used to form the entity in which the business or practice is operated.

- ✔ Partnership and/or buy/sell agreements, or shareholder buy/sell, and so forth.

- ✔ Listing of all consummated buy-ins and buyouts. If anyone has been bought out or if someone recently purchased an interest in the business, these transactions could be vitally important in valuing the business.

- ✔ Copy of all leases and other significant contracts in effect at the valuation date.

- ✔ Your wife's curriculum vitae.

- ✔ Fee or price schedules of the practice or business in place during the past five years.

- ✔ Listing of staff with a description of their work experience and length of time associated with the practice or business.

- ✔ Depreciation schedule of fixed assets.

- ✔ Aging of accounts receivable for different years.

- ✔ Detail listing of prepaid expenses as of the most recent balance sheet.

- ✔ Listing of all benefits and expenses paid for by the practice on behalf of the members of the firm.

2. *Job performance in the business or practice.* Analyze the role and the day-to-day performance and importance of your wife in her practice or business. Consider the following questions:

- ✔ What hours does she work?

- ✔ How are these demonstrated?

✔ Is this physical data consistent with your understanding of your spouse's work habits?

✔ Are her work hours consistent with any personal calendar?

✔ What duties are performed?

✔ How extensive is her overall practice responsibility?

✔ Is she the rainmaker, an insider, or both?

✔ How much of the practice's revenues does she generate?

3. *Profile of the practice or business.* To make judgment calls as to capitalization rate, revenue multiples, and other important factors, your appraiser will need information on the practice or business. It is important to understand the operations of the practice. Who or what produces revenue? What is the difference between what is billed and what is collected per hour? What is the role of the support staff? Is there revenue generation at that level? How much interaction is there between the client and the support staff? In addition to these questions, consider the following factors, all of which affect the value of a practice:

✔ Desirability of the location of the practice. For example, a short-term lease may be less valuable than a long-term lease or ownership, if the location is critical. However, a short-term lease from a related party may be more secure than a longer lease from an unrelated party.

✔ The degree of specialization in the practice. For example, if your wife is a physician with a primary care practice, where the same patients return for periodic examinations or treatments (e.g., dentistry, opthamology, podiatry, general internal medicine), then a greater value for goodwill is typically assumed. This assumption should, however, be analyzed in light of the profitability of the practice, consistency of historical revenues, and other factors.

✓ Competition. The number of practitioners in the same specialty in the area served by the practice will influence the value of your wife's practice.

✓ Diversity of practice. A highly specialized practice may be more risky (depending on the specialty and competition). But it may also produce greater fees. In other instances, a diverse practice may be more secure. This could be especially true in light of pending legislative developments affecting the medical profession.

✓ Potential to retain the client base and to attract additional clients. First the source of clients must be clarified. For a podiatrist, local advertising may be key. For a surgical specialty, physician referral may be the primary source of patients.

✓ Your wife's reputation among colleagues and referral sources.

✓ The practice's history of retention of key employees, if any.

✓ If a medical practice, the nature and type of hospital facilities available; staff privileges; requirements/credentials required.

✓ Status and trends of the specialty of the practice.

✓ Significant economic and demographic trends in the area.

✓ Ownership of the office telephone number, as compared to a license subject to limitations.

✔ Service mix, client base, and nature of operations. A very specialized service may produce higher fees, but may also require higher costs.

✔ Gross receipts, net profits, overhead, and collection ratios. A more predictable revenue stream is a positive attribute for valuation purposes. Consideration must also be given to the possibility that routine services sometimes may be performed readily by any trained professional. This could reduce the value of goodwill since it may be easier for patients or clients to patronize a different practice.

✔ If a medical practice, the patient base should be considered: volume and quality of patients; the number and nature of procedures performed; patient age mix and demographics; and who the payor is: patient, Medicare, Medicaid, or a third-party reimbursement?

✔ Earning stream of the practice and how it compares to the period that would be required to build a similar earnings stream from a new practice.

4. *Client or Customer Profile.* The value of a professional practice or business will vary depending on the type and number of customers served and their longevity with the firm. Therefore, you should consider the following factors in evaluating the quality of the existing client base:

✔ Industry diversification.

✔ Geographic distribution.

✔ Breakdown by gender.

✔ Length of service by the practice.

✔ Maturity of the company.

✔ Record of payment for service fees.

✔ Growth potential.

✔ Sources of new clients.

✔ Extent and kind of referral.

✔ Relationship with the staff and principals of the firm.

✔ Type of services rendered.

Also, keep in mind that the mere facts out of context of the practice itself can be quite misleading.

5. *Industry data.* Depending on the nature of the particular practice or business, several sources of industry data can be helpful in evaluating the particular practice. Start by reading magazines and newsletters for the particular industry. Try to identify an industry trade organization and contact them for statistical data as to values of similar practices or businesses.

Rule #113. Get Your Own Business Appraised

Equity in a small business is an asset of your marriage. Different states will treat it differently. A host of often complex issues can be raised. What date should the valuation be determined? What portion of the business is included? This could depend on a determination of the portion you own in case you have partners. It could also depend on the value of the business as of the date of your marriage if you had started the business before getting married. If the business started before the marriage, there may be a reduction for the value of the business at the date of the marriage so that you're only looking at the increase in the value of the business during the marriage, advises Rob Schlegel, of Houlihan Valuation Advisers, Indianapolis, Indiana.

Business value is not only important for property settlement purposes, it can also impact child support. If your business (which is nonliquid) is a substantial asset and if you're paying child support, and if the court accepts a high valuation figure for your business, you can have a serious financial problem. Your ex may get liquid assets such as cash and securities, whereas you get a business that is not liquid and a large alimony and child support obligation. You could be pressed. This is why it's important to present the case properly. You need a competent and credible valuation expert. You need to fashion an arrangement that won't force you into contempt for not making required payments to your ex-wife.

Business valuation is not an exact science. Your closely held retail store, professional practice, or other business can be hard to value. Many assumptions are involved. As the assumptions, even with small differences between your appraiser and your wife's appraiser, are multiplied through the valuation process, the ultimate impact on the final valuation figure can be tremendous. "In many cases that go to trial the two experts are on different planets. You need someone with the technical and professional background, but who is also a good witness to protect your interests," warns Paul L. Feinstein, Esq., of Chicago, Illinois.

Although it's always better to settle valuation cases without a trial, because such trials can be costly and it's tough to know how a judge will decide, this is not always possible. "You can't negotiate with terrorists. When the issue is valuation and the experts for you and your wife are miles apart on valuation, you may even be willing to give her 50 percent of the value to settle. But if your appraiser values your business at $1 million, and your wife's expert values it at $5 million, you can't settle," says Feinstein.

So what can you do? "For starters, spend the money and get formal appraisals with detailed reports because a good report is more likely to carry weight in the negotiation process. Also, values tend to change over time and you can shortchange yourself if you don't consider this," advises Amy J. Amundsen, Esq., of Memphis, Tennessee.

Does it pay to fight the requests for information on your business made by your ex's expert. Don't fight to hide basic data that will have to be disclosed. You don't need to volunteer information in a deposition, however: if the other side doesn't ask for something, don't offer it. "Don't hold back with respect to the historical operational data and even good things that have happened in the business. Don't hold back information about the risks. These are almost always ultimately made available, it can often just run up a legal fee fighting over what you'll almost invariably give."

But the philosophy in the legal profession is that if you make things onerous enough, the other side may give up. In most cases, though, it's just more costly because you will have to fork over these documents anyway. So be sure you agree with what your attorney is trying to do in this regard. Your attorney may be encouraging you to disclose something that may actually help you. Also, if you don't disclose, you risk having your ex-wife and her attorney assume something worse. Don't destroy documents. The assumption made by your wife's appraiser could be far worse. "I think you should talk to your valuation expert and tell them as much about the business as you can without withholding information. If you think there are relevant elements, you should volunteer it. Most attorneys will advise you 'don't say anything.' The expert is really not an advocate for your wife. The expert who favors either side too much will lose his or her own professional reputation. Experts are not advocates. If they are, they won't be around as credible experts very long. Experts are advocates for their own opinions, not your side or your wife's side. So, opt for an expert who is well known and has a reputation [at stake]," suggests Rob Schlegel, of Houlihan Valuation Advisers, Indianapolis, Indiana.

The traditional attorney views the business valuation as one of many pieces of evidence to be evaluated as part of the overall process. Now there are more attorneys to address the complexity of valuation issues. If you have two experts produce business valuations, consider a mediation by a third expert. For small businesses, mediation is especially useful. Try to identify differences and deal with them. For smaller businesses try to hire a neutral expert for both you and your ex—a joint assignment. Each party can always hire another expert. Why not start that way and try it first.

How do you choose an appraiser? You want someone certified because certified appraisers keep current, have specified minimum experience, and have passed a test. Some certifications are more stringent than others. Some have been easy to get. The best certifications include ASA—Accredited Senior Appraiser in Business Valuation by American Society of Appraisers; or CPA/ABV—Accredited in Business Valuation by the American Institute of Certified Public Accountants (AICPA). A third credential is the Certified Business Appraiser through the Institute of Business Appraisers (IBA), which is not as well known but has strong requirements. IBA focuses mostly on small businesses. You want your wife to get a certified appraiser, even if you're paying the cost. "If you get some yahoo who doesn't know what they are doing, they can cause a lot of harm," warns Schlegel. The certification is not a guarantee. There are also some excellent appraisers who are not certified.

Rule #114. Use Clever Approaches to Quickly and Inexpensively Value a Business

Valuation of a closely held business is a complex and costly process, and due diligence is time consuming. If the business is not that valuable, or if you and your spouse can act together, there may be some creative ways to value the business for less cost and hassle than by hiring an independent appraiser.

In some cases there may exist facts that support a quick, relatively inexpensive, and surprisingly convincing valuation by using a time-tested operations research technique called regression analysis. This technique is not new to the valuation arena, having a history of use in valuing assets such as royalty streams, licenses, and other assets. It has, however, been overlooked by many matrimonial attorneys.

Many closely held businesses are appraised at times prior to a divorce process for valid business purposes, such as the following:

☛ Loan transaction.

☛ Prospective sale.

☛ Fairness opinion for a possible public offering.

☛ Negotiations between shareholders to buy one another out.

☛ Appraisal for estate planning purposes.

Where you have several prior valuations, but no current figure, regression analysis can provide a quick estimate of value. Depending on the underlying nature of the business (e.g., the relationship of revenues to costs), the valuation can be quite reasonable. For example, in a business characterized as an established company with steady history of continuous growth, this methodology could yield reasonable results. If, as revenues grow and fixed costs for production and facilities remain relatively constant (because there is no need to increase plant size), the value of the business predicted by the regression method should even be conservative. Regression analysis can provide a little bonus: because the valuations are all based on those done by the spouse in the business (or by third parties hired by the spouse), it can be difficult to dispute them. The spouse would logically have to demonstrate a marked change in the fundamental cost structure of the business to dispute the methodology.

Regression analysis illustrates a relationship between one variable and another. Through statistical analysis, an equation is derived that quantifies this relationship. This equation is used as a tool to estimate values of a dependent variable, based on known values of an independent variable. In a divorce process, regression analysis can be used to illustrate a relationship between sales of the business and the value of the company. The regression equation could use revenues of the business as the independent variable and valuations of the business as the dependent variable. The "revenue" variable is plotted along the horizontal axis of a graph, and the "value of company" (Y) variable is plotted along the vertical axis of the graph. Then for any date, revenues can be determined from tax returns, internal accounting programs, and so forth and simply plugged into the formula to determine the value at the date desired. The process is simple, inexpensive, and depending on the particular facts, reasonably accurate.

Rule #115. Review All Appraisals and Valuations of Significant Assets

Regardless of whom you hire to appraise your business (or any other asset), the appraiser should provide you with a comprehensive and detailed draft report. Review the draft report and in particular all assumptions the appraiser has made. You may want to share a draft report with your ex-wife. If it is stamped "draft," it has some flexibility. In many matrimonial cases, the problem is that each side gets its own appraisal report in a fancy cover, and then the positions are frozen and the attorneys will do everything possible to make sure that their side's opinion controls. It's better to have experts meet over "draft" reports; they can often resolve the issues without protracted litigation.

The industry has a review process, the Uniform Standards of Professional Appraisal Practice (USPAP). There are also standards by the America Society of Appraisers and the Institute of Business Appraisers. There are references in these as to how another expert's report should be reviewed. If your wife selects an appraiser first, when the report comes in, you can hire another appraiser to review it and there are procedures to identify the differences.

Appraisers going through this process with draft reports will address many of the usual games they see in the valuation of closely held business interests. If these are present, it may be best for you to have the appraisers try to negotiate a settlement on the valuation, because these issues coming out at trial will not help you.

Many valuation experts who have done a lot of divorce work understand that when they are engaged by the wife's attorney and they talk to the husband who owns the business, they expect to hear a tale of woe about how poorly the business is doing. The reason is that the business is viewed as an asset the man will keep when the assets are divided. The idea that the man keeps the business and the wife keeps the house and investments is still largely true. These tales of woe are classic and expected. After the divorce, that business often makes a dramatic recovery. This can be in your interest as it will make for a lower appraisal; the backlash is that if you're discovered, you can lose any credibility in the eyes of the judge, which can hurt you in the entire trial.

The valuation date can present another issue to address concerning the value of your business. Many states value as of the date of filing for divorce, or let the judge choose a date between filing and the hearing. So running the business down after you file probably doesn't do you much good anyway; the business may be valued as of the date you filed.

Rule #116. Report All Business Deposits Properly

If you commingle business and personal transactions, the judge may disregard all your records and instead direct a forensic accountant to reconstruct cash flow based on your lifestyle.

A less severe but more common problem arises if you pocket cash from business transactions without reporting it as income. This could happen in several ways. If your customers pay cash, you might be tempted to skim some instead of depositing it. Don't do it: This can often be easily identified by your wife's forensic accountant. The accountant simply analyzes the cost of goods sold and other common financial ratios for your business over a number of years and compares those ratios to industry average ratios for similar companies. All this information is readily available, and it can easily and quickly demonstrate that unreported cash or other abnormalities are present.

Another approach one husband used unsuccessfully was to simply keep as cash a portion of every bank deposit for business receipts. "The husband destroyed all copies of bank deposit slips that reflected the cash amounts," explains Ginita Wall, a San Diego forensic accountant. "To his surprise, all we did was have the bank provide copies of the deposit slips it retained. He was caught red-handed."

The moral of the preceding stories is that you should probably come clean. You won't be the first husband to try any of a whole bag of tricks to reduce the value of your business. Most forensic accountants have seen most of the tricks lots of times. Not only will your shenanigans be adjusted back, but you'll have lost any credibility. When other issues arise later, which side is the judge likely to think more accurate?

Rule #117. Don't "Cook the Books" of Your Closely Held Business

Closely held businesses and professional practices present many planning opportunities for you. They also can create costly and complex problems. The following illustrates just one issue: how far you can go with manipulating business figures.

Your matrimonial attorney cannot advise you to hide assets or to not disclose assets you have. But your matrimonial attorney can send you to another attorney specializing in corporate law to examine the way the corporation operates to determine if it is best positioned financially for your divorce. There may be steps such as purchasing more equipment, increasing inventory levels, taking on more business debt, or otherwise reducing liquidity to affect the valuation of the businesses potentially. This planning may not always be picked up by your wife's appraiser, or an agreement may be reached before it's found, observes Lynne Strober, Esq., of Mandelbaum, Salsburg, Gold, Lazris, Discenza & Steinberg in West Orange, New Jersey. However, if these games are caught not only will adjustments be made, but your wife's experts will dig deeper to uncover other manipulations and you will lose any credibility with the court. Is it worth it?

Similarly, when you fill out the case information sheet for your case with the financial data, you don't have to list assets that you don't have at that time. A case information sheet is a standard disclosure statement; it may have a different name in your state, but the information is similar: full disclosure of all assets, debts, and living expenses.

How far can you go with this type of planning? If the changes you make are not supported by some business reason or are out of sync with historic data, you should expect problems. For example, you can't increase your inventory levels to 150 percent of historical average and not expect that they will be noticed! Expect your wife's forensic expert, at minimum, to examine the historical business data for three to five years—and if there are unusual circumstances or a problem with the data presented, more years may be required. The expert will analyze the ratios of the different income and expense categories over these years looking for any obvious manipulations, inconsistencies, or items that appear out of line. Further, expect the expert to obtain industry data using Bureau of Labor Department data, industry data from the American Institute of CPAs, and industry data from any industry trade group to analyze and compare your data. So, any items that are out of line with the historical data for your business or from industry or expected data will probably be identified and require an explanation from you.

If you undertake this type of planning, you must weigh the risks. If your ex-wife's forensic accountant demonstrates that you've systematically restructured your business transactions to look bad for valuation purposes, not only will these machinations be undone, but they may be undone with a vengeance, resulting in a valuation that is more unfair to you than had you taken no actions. You may even be required to pay for the extra costs your ex's expert incurs in ferreting out your scheme.

Rule #118. Beware of Business Activities That Can Adversely Affect Your Access to Assets

If you're working, particularly as a professional, or if you own a closely held business, and if your wife is either a stay-at-home wife or works in a position with little financial risk (e.g., a teacher) you might have transferred key personal assets, such as your house and securities account, to her name. If you're now heading into divorce, you could face considerable difficulties. Theoretically, the ownership (title) of assets shouldn't matter. This is because equitable distribution looks to achieve an equitable division of assets, no matter which spouse owns them. However, while you are going through the divorce process, if you've put key assets such as your home and investments in your wife's name, you could at minimum face a substantial tactical disadvantage. You may be able to transfer some assets back in your name and take out more insurance. At least get lines of credit in place to give you cash.

Rule #119. Don't Pay Your Lawyer from Your Business

Way too many husbands think they are way too clever, so they pay lots of personal expenses from their business. These self-anointed "CPAs" think they're smart because they're going to get a tax break and reduce business profits so that the business will be worth less when their wife's forensic accountant values it. "Too often men pay their divorce attorney out of the business and charge the cost to 'legal fees,'" observes Ginita Wall, a San Diego forensic accountant. "For starters, you don't get a tax deduction for divorce legal expenses. It's a personal expense and not a business expense. Secondly, you could make it possible for your wife's attorney to join the business as part of the divorce proceeding. If the business paid your lawyer, shouldn't the business be subject to even more scrutiny? This might give your ex's attorney even more access to business information." Just what you wanted. Worst of all, when your wife's forensic accountant sees this level of blatant fraud, it will encourage the accountant to dig further to see what other buried treasures you've hidden.

The judge is also unlikely to be impressed with a long list of inappropriate personal expenses hidden to reduce your wife's likely property settlement. One of the most extreme cases uncovered a $25,000 necklace for hubby's mistress, buried in the cost of goods sold in an advertising firm. True, because the business made millions of dollars of purchases, the husband might have gotten away with it. However, the methodical husband had saved copies of these personal purchases in a locked file cabinet in his home office. Little did he know, but Mrs. Sherlock Holmes had the key and knew how to use the copy machine! His wife had cleverly copied all his personal files before the couple split.

8

Tax Tips and Traps to Avoid

Rule #120. Don't Forget the Tax Man

Income and estate taxes are critical to negotiating any property settlement. Consider the following situations.

If low-basis assets are transferred to you (e.g., a share of stock that you purchased for $1 that is now worth $100), you will have to recognize this gain if you take this asset and later sell it. Be certain that you have an accountant calculate the computed tax cost associated with every asset. "People still overlook the tax basis issue," observes Sidney Kess, a New York City tax attorney and CPA. "Although it's common knowledge to anyone familiar with taxes, many couples try to make agreements on their own to save money and overlook this. The tax cost can prove far greater than the cost to have hired a skilled matrimonial attorney."

Different types of gains are also taxed differently. For example, if you trade your medical practice for your stock portfolio, you keep the practice and your wife gets the stock—your wife can make out tremendously. The income you will earn from your practice will be taxed as ordinary income at rates of up to 40 percent. This includes the realization of the accounts receivable, which may be a significant portion of the asset value. If your wife sells the stock she gets to raise cash she'll pay less tax, if any. The stock portfolio, however, may generate capital gains taxed at only 20 percent on any appreciation.

If instead you had traded your medical practice for the house, the net of tax disparity between you and your ex could even be more unfair to you. Remember that certain assets can avoid taxes altogether, such as the marital residence if properly handled. You and your wife are permitted (subject to some complex rules) to sell and avoid tax on up to $250,000 of gain in the marital residence. The gain avoided can be up to $500,000 if you plan properly before the divorce.

If you pay alimony to your spouse, it is deductible for federal income tax purposes by you, whereas child support is not. This must be carefully evaluated when trading off greater or lesser alimony for a lesser or greater property settlement. The tax differences can be substantial, so consider the varying tax rates that you each face in determining how to allocate the various payments between alimony and child support. You don't want to get whipsawed into a lousy tax deal by overlooking important tax considerations. Also, if through careful planning of the divorce settlement the federal fisc can bear some of the cost of your settlement through tax savings, you, your ex, and the kids can all benefit. It is not a zero sum game.

Retirement assets pose special tax problems. Many husbands often want to keep retirement assets in lieu of other assets. Deferred compensation and retirement benefits are taxable; they should keep this in mind and consider the posttax value, warns Amy J. Amundsen, Esq., of Memphis, Tennessee.

Stock options are another significant asset that has received a lot of press lately and is rife with tax problems. Don't draw any conclusions about options without discussing the current law in your state with your attorney. In some states, all nonvested options are considered marital property, even if you have to work after the divorce to keep them. Some states take a hybrid approach, saying a portion is marital property, a portion not.

Rule #121. Tell Uncle Sam about the Split

Tell the IRS as soon as you split up and move out. File Form 8822 "Change of Address" to report your new address. This is vitally important so that you will receive copies of any tax notices that may affect you. Call 1-800-TAX-FORM to order a copy.

Rule #122. Split Your Portfolio to Save Taxes

If your divorce agreement requires the division of a stock portfolio or mutual fund, try not to sell and divide the proceeds because you may trigger a large capital gains tax. "Instead, consider simply dividing up the account in the required proportions. Then either you or your ex can do what you wish with your now separate accounts and the other of you is not going to get hit with a capital gains tax cost if you didn't want to sell," notes Saul M. Simon, CFP, financial adviser with Allmerica Investment Management Company, Inc., Edison, New Jersey. Try to get your lawyer to negotiate a split on the account instead of a cash payment, which creates tax problems. This can save brokerage costs on reinvesting as well. With a bit of paperwork, you can even divide assets so that the built-in capital gains are also divided relatively equally.

Here's another tip to make life easier. If you're splitting an account, have your ex open an account in her name at the same brokerage firm. Do the split there first; your ex-wife can then transfer the account anywhere she wants later. This will save lots of administrative headaches compared with trying to transfer half of the securities from your account and firm A to her account at firm B. "It's always easier to complete an interfirm transfer when the account title matches," suggests Simon.

Rule #123. Know the Special Tax Laws That May Affect the Sale of Your Former Marital Residence

A home can not only be one of your largest assets but one with a substantial tax cost as well. "Under the old house sale rules when you had a case where the husband had a girlfriend and moved out of the home, the husband would try to claim that he was entitled to the $125,000 exclusion (if he was over age 55) and a rollover of any gain into a purchase of a new home. Courts had taken the position that since the husband had moved out of the house it wasn't his residence and he couldn't get the tax benefits. Under recent legislation if the husband moves out of the house, but if his wife or ex-wife is still living there, he can be deemed to qualify for special home sale tax benefits," explains Sidney Kess, a New York City attorney and CPA. "Under these new rules, if the husband can meet a test of being deemed to have lived in the home for two of the five years before sale, the house will qualify as his residence and the special tax breaks on home sales will be available. "If you live in the house for two of the last five years its deemed to still be your principal residence and you can qualify for the new $250,000 exclusion. Even if husband is out of the house he might meet the test. This rule makes it more valuable for husbands to keep an interest in the marital residence.

If your former marital residence is to be sold, complications will affect tax planning. You must use the house as a residence for a certain number of years to qualify for tax breaks. If one spouse (say your ex) is granted exclusive use of the residence pursuant to a separation agreement, divorce decree, or other instrument, that use will be credited to you for purposes of determining if you meet the use and ownership requirements to qualify for favorable home sale tax benefits. For many younger clients, this may be of little practical benefit if the children of the marriage are quite young such that the time period is often insufficient.

Exercise caution to be certain that the usage is mandated by a qualifying agreement. If not, it will not be credited to the spouse not residing in the house. The timing of each spouse's use and ownership should be considered to assure the maximum qualification for the exclusion.

It may be advantageous to delay the divorce or the common filing of separate tax returns, to assure that the full $500,000 exclusion is available. In the context of a divorce settlement if the house is transferred to one spouse, that transferee spouse may treat the house as if he or she had owned it during the period it was owned by the transferor spouse.

Rule #124. Understand How Payments to Your Ex Will Be Taxed

Most divorce settlements comprise three general types of payments: property settlements, alimony or maintenance, and child support. The tax treatment of alimony and property settlements is substantially different. For example, you can claim a deduction for alimony payments but not for a property settlement. To prevent payors from manipulating property settlements to make them look like deductible alimony payments, the tax laws provide certain tests. In general terms these tests try to prevent you from treating a property settlement (which you can't deduct) as alimony (which you can deduct). Any payments the law treats like disguised property settlements are considered "excess" alimony and will be taxed as a property settlement.

Rule #125. If You Want Payments to Your Ex to Be Deductible, Follow the Rules

If you want alimony or maintenance payments to your ex to be deductible for tax purposes, you must meet the following requirements:

- ✔ The payments must be made under a decree of divorce, legal separation agreement, or a decree of support.

- ✔ The agreement must require that the payments cease on your ex's death.

- ✔ You and your ex must live in separate households.

- ✔ You can't continue to file a joint income tax return with your wife.

- ✔ The payments cannot be for child support. If the payments are reduced based on a contingency related to the child (e.g., the child graduates college or attains the age of 18, etc.), they're child support not alimony.

✔ The payments must be in cash (or by check). The payment has to be in cash, not property such as furniture. You can pay bills, (e.g., to your wife's doctors) directly and still claim a deduction for alimony if the payments are requested by your ex and are in place of alimony. So you can pay for insurance premiums, mortgage payments, and other items and qualify to deduct the payment.

✔ The payment cannot be a property settlement.

Where there are excess alimony payments, the husband must include the excess payments in his gross income in the third post-separation year. The wife is permitted a corresponding deduction. The recapture rules will not be triggered where the fluctuations in the payments are not within your control.

In general, where the stipulated payments are to be reduced based on a contingency relating to the child (e.g., the child's age or status) the payments are characterized as child support and not alimony. The tax consequence of a payment being characterized as child support instead of alimony (maintenance) is that you, as the payor, will not receive any tax deduction for the payment, and your ex-wife will not have to report any portion of the payment as taxable income.

The tax considerations of structuring a settlement so that certain payments will be properly characterized as either alimony or child support are simple. One is taxable/deductible, and the other is not. It will, in part, be a question of negotiating for the benefit of the tax result you want. Your accountant can assist in such negotiations by projecting the after-tax result for you under various scenarios and various assumptions about tax rates and other factors specific to your case.

Rule #126. Tax Considerations of Property Settlements

The objective of the tax rules governing property settlements is to make property transfers that implement a divorce settlement tax free, and to make the tax results of divorce settlements uniform no matter what state the parties reside in. No gain or loss will be recognized where one individual transfers property to a spouse, or a former spouse, where the transfer is treated as incident to the divorce. The transfer can be either directly or in trust.

A simple example illustrates this basic rule and the critical importance of properly planning for tax consequences. Suppose you are negotiating a divorce settlement, and your only two marital assets are $200,000 in cash and some ABC stock purchased by your wife prior to the marriage. The stock is also worth $200,000, but your wife paid only $10,000 for it many years ago. If you were to receive the stock and your wife the cash in the divorce settlement, you would both be economically equal. However, the stock carries with it a potential tax cost. When you attempt to sell the stock to obtain cash, you could incur a tax cost of approximately $38,000 [($200,000 − $10,000) × 20%]. Thus, you will have really only received $162,000 in value. So perhaps a fairer settlement would be to give each spouse $181,000 [($162,000 + $200,000) × 50%]. The situation might also become far more complicated. If one spouse had large capital loss carry forwards, there might not be any tax cost on the sale of the stock. A capital loss is when you sell stock for less than you paid. If the losses are too large in one year you may not be able to deduct all of them in that year but instead deduct part in a later year. This is called a carry forward. Perhaps the transferee spouse, your wife, has

178

sufficient other income and will not have to dispose of the stock in the foreseeable future.

Suppose the asset were real estate, which could qualify for a tax-free exchange under other tax law provisions. Would the result be the same as in the previous scenario? The key point is that the inherent tax cost created by a transfer of property subject to the mandatory Internal Revenue Code Section 1041 nonrecognition rules must be analyzed. This analysis must consider all the relevant facts and circumstances. If these issues could affect the settlement, get competent professional advice before signing.

Rule #127. Split Your IRA to Avoid Tax Problems

Everyone knows that withdrawing money out of an IRA before age 59½ can result in income tax costs and a 10 percent penalty, too. There are a few exceptions from this costly result, one being for division of an IRA as part of a divorce settlement. If you transfer part of your IRA account to your wife under your divorce decree, there will be no tax cost to either you or your ex. Your ex should set up her own IRA accounts and you should have the required amount directly wired from your IRA account to hers.

Rule #128. Get All Necessary Records from Your Spouse as Part of the Divorce Settlement

Be sure that you have copies of all pertinent tax records and that the divorce or separation agreement requires your ex to provide these to you. The best approach is to have important documents attached to the agreement as an exhibit, or at least expressly listed in the agreement. If you need tax records after everything is signed and done, why should your ex cooperate? And although she might be willing to cooperate, if she has to dig through dozens of boxes in the attic to find a particular record, will she be willing to bother? So be sure to get the records you need before your divorce is final.

Rule #129. Claim Your Children as Dependents for Tax Savings

Who can claim the children as dependents for tax purposes is an issue in many divorces. The tax benefits from claiming a child as your dependent can be valuable and the deductions may be available for many years. If you have several children and pay high state and local taxes, this tax benefit can become significant. Therefore, it is important to understand the basic requirements for determining how you can qualify for the dependency exemption for each of the children involved. Be certain to review the allocation of dependency exemptions with the attorney handling your case, because the language your attorney inserts in the separation or divorce agreement may determine your right to claim exemptions.

The general rule for determining which parent can claim a dependency exemption is simple. Where the parents are divorced, separated, or living apart at all times during the last six months of the calendar year, the parent having actual custody over the particular child for the greater part of the year will generally be entitled to claim the exemption for that child. For this rule to apply, the parents must together have custody of the child for more than half of the year and must together provide over half of the child's support.

There are, however, a number of exceptions to this basic general rule. If the custodial parent expressly waives or releases the right to claim a dependency exemption for a child, the other (noncustodial) parent may claim the exemption. The custodial parent must file Form 8332 declaring that she won't claim the exemption for one or more calendar years. The noncustodial parent can attach this form to his tax return and can then claim the exemption for that year. Thus, if your wife has custody but you are in a higher tax bracket, you should consider specifically negotiating that the divorce agreement gives you the deduction if the other requirements are met.

If you and your ex have a joint custody arrangement, your separation agreement should specify which parent will be entitled to the exemptions and that the other parent waives any right to claim the exemption and will provide any future forms or filings (such as Form 8332) necessary to implement this arrangement.

If you didn't pay over half of the child's support, you might still salvage the dependency deduction if you can qualify for a multiple support agreement. This requires that you pay more than 10 percent of the child's support and no other person paid over half. All people who paid more than 10 percent of the child's support must sign IRS Form 2120.

Finally, however, you should review with your accountant whether phaseouts of these tax exemptions will eliminate any benefit you might receive.

Rule #130. Don't Automatically File a Joint Income Tax Return

If you file a joint income tax return with your new wife and your ex-wife re-petitions the court asking for more money, that joint return with your new wife could be analyzed by your ex-wife's attorney. What portion of the income on that joint return (and hence what portion of the assets generating that income) belongs to you? In some instances, especially if re-petitioning is likely, you should discuss with your matrimonial attorney and accountant the possibility of filing "married filing separately" with your new wife. In this way, if your ex-wife re-petitions the court, your new wife's earnings, dividends, business income, and so forth, should not be part of the analysis. This could eliminate the difficulty of proving that something is not yours. Carefully weigh the additional income tax costs you may incur by doing this. Your accountant can provide you with a calculation.

Rule #131. Consider Filing Separate Tax Returns Even before You Divorce

If divorce is even on the horizon, consider filing separate tax returns. It will minimize the complexity of dealing with a future IRS audit and minimize the need to deal with complex financial matters with your ex. The only reason to consider a joint return is if the tax cost of a separate return is too costly. The best approach is to have your accountant calculate the tax both ways and then make a decision. With almost all tax returns being completed by computer, this is a quick and simple task.

For you and your soon-to-be ex-wife to qualify to file a tax return as married and filing jointly, you must meet the tax law definitions of "married." The determination of marital status is made at the close of the tax year. Where a couple is considered to be married under local state law rules at the end of the tax year, they will be considered married for federal income tax purposes. The fact that you are physically separated at year-end is not determinative that you were not married for federal tax purposes. The fact that the two of you have executed a separation agreement is also not necessarily sufficient to characterize you as not married. If the two of you are legally separated under a decree of divorce or of separate maintenance, you will not be considered married. To qualify as a "decree of separate maintenance," the court decree must order the couple to live separate and apart. A husband and wife separated under an interlocutory decree of divorce retain the relationship of husband and wife until the decree becomes final.

Certain married persons living apart will be considered not married for federal tax purposes. To qualify, you must meet the following requirements:

- File a separate tax return.

- Maintain as your home a household that constitutes for more than one-half of the year the principal place of abode of a child for whom you are claiming a dependency deduction.

- Furnish over one-half of the cost of maintaining such household during the tax year.

183

✔ Make sure your wife is not a member of such household during the last six months of the tax year.

Rule #132. Come Clean on Tax Problems before They Bite You in the Back

Tax shenanigans are no exception to the rule to go clean. If you haven't reported your full income on your tax return, if you've claimed bogus deductions, or if you've paid personal expenses out of your business, you could face a serious problem of disclosure if your divorce goes to court, cautions Lynne Strober, Esq., of Mandelbaum, Salsburg, Gold, Lazris, Discenza & Steinberg, in West Orange, New Jersey. If you have any of these issues, address them with a tax attorney. If your matrimonial attorney does not have a tax specialist in his or her firm, get an outside expert. You may be able to take steps now to document some of the questionable items. It may even be advisable to file amended returns and go clean.

Rule #133. Change Your W-4 to Reduce Your Tax Withholding and Help Out Cash Flow

"Your divorce can change your entire income tax picture," notes Saul M. Simon, CFP, financial adviser with Allmerica Investment Management Company, Inc., Edison, New Jersey. Your cash flow can be very tight. One often overlooked source of immediate funds is to change the tax withholding at your job. This is done by requesting a new Form W-4 from your employer. Fill it out carefully, noting your new deductions for alimony to reduce the tax to be withheld.

If you have lost your tax deduction for your house, now that your ex lives there and pays the tax, you must plan for your tax picture. You can get a step up on this with Quicken—which offers a cash flow and tax model. Input your new income and expenses and it will help you calculate your estimated tax picture. "It's like a minitax return included in a budget" notes Lori Sackler, Certified Financial Planner in New York City. "Once you get this information, you can adjust your withholding, increase or decrease your estimated tax liability, and review your investment picture in light of this tax picture," she suggests.

9

Preparing for Divorce Court

Rule #134. File First: The Early Bird Gets the Worm

The first person to file usually has a clear plan of action. You should first spend adequate time investigating your choice of lawyers, as discussed in Chapter 2. Then (as discussed in Chapter 3), you want to examine all your financial records making sure your wife's name has been eliminated on all credit cards and bank accounts, so long as you are the only one placing money in such accounts. Again, be sure that your actions are really necessary and that by cancelling credit cards you won't be escalating the situation.

Depending on the laws in your state, there may or may not be an advantage to filing for divorce first. But there could be a vitally important reason to do so: there may be more than one court in your state in which to file for divorce. There may be pros and cons to having your particular case heard in a particular court. Perhaps the judges in one court are more experienced in complex commercial matters and the key family asset is your complex business holdings. Perhaps the judges in one of the potential courts have leaned to a particular type of settlement. Ask your attorney, because these are all technical legal issues you shouldn't try to figure out on your own.

In addition to the preceding planning procedures, there is the element of surprise and intimidation—but be sure this is what you want and what is really appropriate for the circumstances. Don't forget that your goal should be to give your wife equal or equitable distribution of assets (as required by the laws in your state) unless she has committed some grave moral offense, like having an affair with your best friend. Even if she has committed something you find morally horrific, the laws in your state may not change what she is still entitled to by way of financial settlements. This is one of the potentially worst situations in a divorce, the type of scenario that can easily escalate out of control. This is when you believe that your ex has committed unforgivable acts and should be punished (or vice versa), but the law views the situation differently. Exercise caution.

The element of surprise and intimidation may be appropriate to offset similar tactics by your wife and/or her lawyer. You are gaining leverage so that when all is said and done, the split is 50/50 rather than 30/70 or more in your wife's favor. Again, be sure that you've thoroughly reviewed all of the pros and cons of this type of action with your attorney and other advisers before committing to it.

Rule #135. Review All Facts and Your Testimony to Prepare for the Trial

You can take several steps to bolster your effectiveness as a credible witness:

Build your resume for added credibility. This can be done by becoming active in charitable and civic organizations, your children's school, and so forth.

Before the trial prepare carefully with your attorney, and carefully review all facts, arguments, and issues well in advance of the trial date. Be certain to review with your attorney any applicable rules of evidence and court procedure with which you should be familiar. You must be thoroughly familiar with all the facts of the case. You should have some understanding of the law and technical issues involved even though experts, and not you, will testify about them. Such preparation is critical to your credibility as a witness.

Review all questions your attorney is likely to ask you on direct examination.

Understand arguments in favor of and against your positions. One of the most effective preparation techniques is to rehearse with your attorney. Many attorneys will conduct a mock examination of you so that you can get a flavor for what the opposing attorney will do. This is often worth the time, expense, and effort. It will help you anticipate some of the many ways your wife's attorney will try to trick you.

If you have a business or professional practice that will be addressed at trial, gain whatever information possible as to the sophistication of the persons who will hear your arguments, and plan your comments appropriately. For example, if you have to testify as to technical aspects of your specialized business, consider preparing a background summary of the business to help describe these technical aspects in simple, nontechnical terminology. Consider using visual aids to clarify your testimony. Clear all these in advance with your attorney.

Rule #136. Know How to Behave on the Stand

Dress conservatively. Your dress and demeanor at trial are critical if your preparation is not to be wasted. Your attire should be professional and conservative.

Act professionally.

Remain cool, calm, and collected. Don't lose your cool no matter what the opposing counsel asks you. Often, getting you to lose your cool is a more important objective of your wife's attorney than is the content of your answers.

Never exceed the bounds of what you can reasonably testify to. Consider the relevance of your prior experience and knowledge. If the question you are asked on the witness stand is beyond the knowledge you have, be honest. If you're not sure, say so.

Expect your wife's attorney to ask tricky questions, to try to fluster and anger you. Don't get caught off guard. Before you go on the stand, realize that your wife and her attorney probably brain stormed about hot buttons of yours to push on the stand. The attorney may try to couch descriptions in the most unfavorable light possible for you. Expect it and be prepared emotionally. Don't lose it on the stand as a result. If you prepare yourself by expecting these things, you'll deal with them better should they occur.

Be consistent and honest. You cannot argue an approach that favors you in one situation and then use a conflicting argument in the next situation simply because it benefits your position. Consistency and honesty are critical. The slightest taint otherwise could destroy your credibility. If there are any factors that could affect your credibility, discuss them completely with your attorney before the trial. For your attorney to hear about your torrid affair for the first time while you're on the witness stand is a tad late for damage control.

If you generally know an answer but would like to look up a record to help refresh your memory, ask to do so before answering incorrectly. For example, if you're asked what the family spends on clothing, you can ask to refresh your recollection by looking at the financial statements that have been submitted by the attorneys in evidence.

Be certain to pay full attention to every detail that the attorney you have hired tells you in preparing you before the trial.

When testifying as to your qualifications concerning your business or professional endeavors, be matter-of-fact but not a braggart. Too many husbands love to talk about themselves. Just remember that your wife's lawyer may intentionally try to get you to "glow" and show off your accomplishments. Your proud responses may come back to haunt you when issues of your compensation, the value of your business, and similar issues are addressed. The solution; don't brag, don't lie, just be factual and direct.

Speak clearly and slowly. Use short sentences and simple words. Speak loudly enough for all in the courtroom to hear your statements. Avoid sounding like a prerehearsed recording. Remember that your comments will be recorded in a court transcript. The typed transcript cannot reflect your sincerity, gestures, facial expressions, or tone of voice. Therefore, concentrate on the words you use since they will be the most critical factor in affecting the outcome of the trial. This is not to say that facial expressions and tone of voice aren't important. They can have a substantial effect at the trial. To have the best impact, be natural, calm, and professional. Avoid overexaggerated gestures or responses. The judge will be watching you and your mannerisms, tone, and facial expressions, and these can have an important bearing on how the judge perceives your honesty and integrity. So even things that aren't "officially" recorded may very well be.

If either attorney raises an objection, hold your response until the matter is resolved. Then respond according to how you are directed by the judge.

On cross-examination (when your wife's attorney questions you), carefully listen to the entire question before responding. If the question is not clear, request that it be repeated or clarified. Many questions you are asked may be tricky or intentionally confusing in the hope of eliciting an incorrect response. If the question can't properly be answered, explain so, or state that it cannot be answered. Frequently, questions are intentionally ambiguous to trip you up or just to fish out what you may say. If a question is unclear, ask for clarification. Do not answer a question until you are certain that you understand exactly what is being asked.

Often questions will be phrased requiring a "yes-no" type response. If a "yes-no" response cannot properly answer the question, say so. Don't be pushed into answering "yes" or "no" to a question that cannot be properly answered with such a reply. When you do answer questions, think through your answer before responding. In some instances, to properly respond, you will be permitted to explain or expand your answer. While you should make every effort to respond to precisely the question asked, you should not permit yourself to be pushed into making an inaccurate statement. In all events, however, your response should be concise and to the point. If the judge becomes impatient and directs you to answer the question with a yes or no, don't become argumentative, answer it. Your lawyer should object if there is a reason to, so don't try to handle your lawyer's role; instead, focus on your role: directly and factually answering the judge's questions and following his or her directions.

Do not volunteer information beyond what is necessary to answer the question. If the question is broad, divide it into logical parts and answer each component. Rambling or disorganized responses can detract from even your strongest positions. To the extent possible, try to anticipate where the attorney conducting the cross-examination is heading. This can enable you to respond to current questions in a manner that lays the groundwork of support for later statements. However, don't lose sight of the question before you.

Be composed. The hotter the questioning, the cooler and calmer you must be. This was the first point for how to testify and is repeated here—it's just too important for you to ignore.

Rule #137. Know What Not to Do as a Witness

Some men are wise guys on the witness stand. They let their ego get in the way. It's a way to exercise control over their ex-wife, bantering with the other lawyer, taking shots at the ex-wife. Women don't tend to do this as much. Be professional and concentrate on the judge, who is your audience. If your wife's attorney is trying to bait you, you can turn it to your advantage if you can express yourself in a dignified manner, advises Paul L. Feinstein, Esq., Chicago, Illinois.

Lynne Gold-Bikin, Esq., of Norristown, Pennsylvania has some additional advice: beware of trying to hide aspects of your character. "One client who alphabetized the baby food in the home was challenged as being an obsessive compulsive. While I was saying he wasn't the husband was organizing my papers at counsel table. In court the judge is always watching you—that's why he sits on the big bench. Be honest!"

Rule #138. Don't Alienate or Antagonize Your Wife's Attorney

It won't help. Your wife's attorney is probably just doing his or her job. You don't want to turn a job into a personal vendetta against you. Greet her attorney with common courtesy. Shake hands. Be polite. Bite your tongue if you have to. If the attorney is acting obnoxiously or inappropriately, it's not your position to set him or her straight. Advise your attorney of the situation and let the attorneys handle it. Your wife's attorney may just be trying to intentionally throw you off guard or to anger you so you won't think as clearly.

Rule #139. If You Don't Know or Don't Remember Something, Just Say So

No witness can ever know or remember the answer to every question. This is especially true if your wife's attorney is attempting to wear you down and "rattle your cage." Focus on each question carefully. If you don't know, or don't remember an answer, say so. Don't guess or fumble around. Not only will it look bad, but a wrong guess could undermine far more of your testimony than just the one item you guessed on.

Rule #140. Keep in Mind That Your Behavior off the Stand Is Also Important

One very angry husband performed like he was going for an Oscar while on the stand. When seated in the courtroom, however, he used to lip-sync curses to the opposing attorney and experts when he was sure the judge wasn't looking. The wife's attorney became fed up with his vile language and gestures and eventually addressed it with the judge. These antics didn't go over well with the court and had a significant impact on the impression and ultimate conclusions of the judge.

Rule #141. Remember Your Children's Birthdays in Court

In presenting a positive image to the judge during cross-examinations in court, you want to remember such salient facts as your wife's birthday, your children's birthdays, what soccer games you attended, the names of your children's pediatrician and other physicians, and other names, dates, and key facts. If you don't know the answers to these questions, this can be used against you.

Lorna Wendt chose Arnold Rutkin, a "take-no-prisoners" attorney, to represent her in her divorce from former GE Capital CEO Gary Wendt. She was seeking a $50 million settlement. During a memorable cross-examination, Rutkin asked Gary for the name of his daughter's pediatrician, but Gary couldn't remember.

197

Then Rutkin asked him to tell the court his wife's birth date. Up on the stand, Gary drew a blank.

Rule #142. Before You Challenge Your Wife, Have Your Ducks (and Facts) in a Row

In one recent custody case in New York state, the divorced couple's child was injured while the husband was traveling on business. The wife didn't tell him about the incident. When the divorce eventually wound its way to trial, the husband and his attorney tried to score points in the custody battle by challenging the wife's responsibility by calling her to task for not having immediately called the husband concerning the incident. She explained her reason was that the father, who was traveling at the time of the accident, didn't react well to hearing about any injuries that occurred to the children.

On cross-examination, the wife's attorney asked the husband if he knew the name of the child's regular pediatrician. He didn't. He asked the husband if he knew the name of the child's optometrist. He didn't. He asked the husband if he knew the name of the plastic surgeon who treated the child's injury. He didn't. The interchange didn't impress the judge with the husband's sincerity or true interest in the child. Apart from trying to use the child as a pawn—which is always wrong—the husband tried to make a point without being prepared, and it backfired on him. Don't pursue a tactic unless you've thought through all the ramifications and reviewed them with your attorney.

10

Getting Back on Your Feet
after the Divorce

Rule #143. Get on with Your Personal Life

"An important contrast between men and women is how they handle life after divorce," observes Stanley Teitelbaum, a psychotherapist in Teaneck, New Jersey. Women say how hard it is to connect in the singles scene, and many claim how much harder it is for women to meet men than for men to meet women. Although much of this is true, it overlooks how hard it is for guys after divorce. Although demographics are in their favor, many men don't know how to go about dating after divorce. Most are uncomfortable and awkward; they aren't sure how to connect, how quickly to move into romance and sex and relationships. Many men find it hard to do and are reluctant to even try.

The key for you to get back on your social feet is to recognize that these are normal phases. If you want to resume your social life and make a connection, you need to tailor your expectations and allow for some disappointment and rejections. You have to be prepared to get turned down. You have to keep trying, and you will make headway. Just knowing that there is a lot of trial and error helps. So don't be put off.

Rule #144. Learn to Deal with Depression and Other Emotions Effectively

Although divorce is more frequently initiated today by women than men, both deal with the feelings of loss. Many women soon experience a feeling of relief, of less constraint, of emancipation to go on with their lives. Men tend to feel loss and get depressed.

201

The depression is not simply feeling down and sad. It's often a clinical depression caused by the loss of what the marriage did represent or could have represented to the man.

Many men are lost without their wives because their wives have become replacements for their earlier relationships to their mothers. For many men, their mothers and then their wives provided planning and structure in the man's life. The wife supplied all these ingredients with a certain kind of nurturing the man came to rely on. Therefore, many men become depressed for an extended period after a divorce because their support system—which they took for granted—has been removed.

How do you get through this? First, you have to realize what is happening. It is helpful to know that this is common, you're not alone. Your reactions are typical. Try a support group that deals with this type of loss, or try other counseling. Make a concerted effort to replace your support system. But keep in mind that too many men react by trying to find a quick replacement (the "rebound" syndrome). Don't feel so inadequate; don't simply try to find a replacement for your wife. Don't succumb to pressure and anxiety. Learn to tolerate that things are different. You have more resources than you know. Think back to before you were married. When you were a bachelor, you probably took care of many things you later depended on your wife to do for you: going to the cleaners, cooking, and so forth. Many men forget how to do these tasks, but you can relearn. In practice, most have forgotten the basics in how to date. Studies indicate that divorcing men commonly go through periods of difficult adjustment often lasting one, two or more years. Shopping, preparing meals, making the bed and general housekeeping are new experiences for some men. The cost of alimony, child support and other possible payments, plus the expense of new living quarters, may not leave much room in the budget for the new life envisioned.

Rule #145. Be Realistic about Your New Financial Picture

Too often men have an idealized view of the postmarriage lifestyle they wish to lead. They visualize independent, nonconforming, possibly even promiscuous and swinging futures being single again. Legal and other fees of the divorce, reduced income as a result of a property settlement, alimony payments, child support, the costs of new living quarters and so on, all have an impact. Put together a budget and get a handle on where you are financially. You may not be able to afford the lifestyle you anticipate. The sooner you bite the bullet and face this reality, the sooner you can begin moving toward financial independence. You need to mentally adjust to your new life. Think of the things you will need and what you can do without. Get real about preparing for the early stages of your divorce.

"Re-evaluate your assets and investments after the divorce," recommends Lori Sackler, Certified Financial Planner in New York City. Review the assets you have now. You may have gotten stuck with investments that are no longer appropriate. Consider your new income needs, obligations from the divorce, "who's responsible for the education bill and how you're going to fund this—it's a big one," she notes.

Rule #146. Take a Postdivorce Financial Planning Checkup

Following your divorce, you have to get your financial picture in order and on track. Get back to the basics; most divorced men tend to overlook simple and obvious things that can have a tremendous impact on them financially, observes Saul M. Simon, CFP, financial planner with Allmerica Investment Management Company, Inc., Edison, New Jersey. Consider the following:

Review and analyze all benefit plans that you have with your employer to confirm beneficiary designations. You may have to change some to meet the requirements of your divorce agreement. You will want to change other benefits that you no longer have to pay to your ex. "So often people leave their ex on as a beneficiary on benefits they no longer have to since they simply forget!" notes Simon.

Review your investment strategies. You may have to take less risk. "An investment checkup is always in order," notes Simon.

Prepare a budget or cash flow analysis even if you've never done one before. Analyze your new financial circumstances, large obligations under the divorce agreement, and any other changes. Many people use a knee-jerk reaction of pulling money out of an IRA or qualified pension plan to meet divorce obligations. "These people have just screwed up big time! The tax consequences can be horrific. You may end up with a whopping income tax bill and a 10 percent penalty if you're under [age] 59½," warns Simon. This is not exactly the financial situation you're looking for when you retire, so plan smart. Prepare or at least review your budget with a planner because there may be better approaches. You can sometimes borrow against a home equity line of credit if you have equity, or you may be able to borrow against remaining insurance policies or in some cases a retirement plan, as an alternative to fund the divorce payments, notes Simon.

No matter how strapped you are, you must begin saving. If you don't start, you'll never regain your financial footing. "It doesn't even matter how little you save, just do like the Nike commercial says: Just Do It!" recommends Simon.

Keep in mind that liquidity is probably a key financial objective. Prior to your divorce, you may have focused on growth, mutual funds, and other longer-term financial strategies and vehicles. However, until you're safely back on your feet, consider liquidity—readily available cash sources—to be a primary objective. "You need to be liquid for all the unexpected expenses you'll be facing as you rebuild your life. These can include car repairs, furnishing a new apartment, a new emergency fund if yours had been decimated in the divorce, and more surprises that are bound to happen," says Simon.

Rule #147. Consider Leasing Assets as an Option to Purchasing Them

"Explore options like leasing a car, computer and other assets if you are cash strapped and cannot come up with the money while you're getting back on your feet," encourages Lori Sackler, Certified Financial Planner in New York City. "However," cautions Sackler, "this is often a more expensive option—so use it as a stopgap and look toward purchasing as soon as you can afford it." Many people erroneously assume leasing is cheaper because businesses commonly use it. However, companies may have tax benefits and clout to negotiate deals that you don't have access to.

Rule #148. Review Your Insurance Protection

The insurance issues you must address, include the following:

Review your group health insurance. Are you required to buy health insurance for your wife and children, just your children, or only yourself? If you don't have to cover some of them, you could save significant dollars.

Correct the coverage of your auto insurance if you only have to pay for one car instead of two. If you're now single, you may want to increase your deductible if you are now the only person driving the car. You may be willing to take a bigger risk to save premium dollars.

Don't forget renter's insurance. If you're now living in an apartment, homeowners' insurance won't help you. You need coverage even if you think your assets are limited. Don't forget that insurance coverage means that the insurance company will pay for legal counsel to defend you if you're sued because someone is injured at your apartment, and so on. You want this even if you don't feel you have assets to lose. Your excess personal liability coverage (umbrella) probably stayed with your ex if she got the house or it may have lapsed during the divorce process. Get new coverage. Review any remaining coverage to make sure you're only paying for what you own, not, for example, the jewelry that your ex-wife now has.

Reevaluate your disability insurance. Reassess the waiting period. If your savings have been emaciated by the divorce, you may need to protect yourself financially by requesting a shorter waiting period before benefits kick in. "However, this has to be weighed against your now tighter cash flow," cautions Simon. Review the financial benefits of your disability insurance. Your divorce settlement may require that you obtain additional disability coverage for your ex-wife and children in the event that your disability prevents you from earning enough money to pay for child support and alimony.

Review your life insurance policies. You will undoubtedly face new requirements under the divorce agreement. If you have excess coverage, then change the beneficiary for the excess to someone other than your ex-wife. If you were overfunding a cash value life insurance policy for future college costs or retirement benefits, those dollars may now be better earmarked for a tax-deductible 401(k) plan. You may have to modify the policy if you can no longer afford the hefty premiums. Evaluate whether a trust should own the policies; if not, there can be a huge tax problem. "Don't count on your matrimonial attorney to have done this properly, it's really a technical matter for an estate planner," cautions Simon.

"You likely will have to meet [some] insurance obligations under your divorce agreement," notes Lori Sackler. Many people jump to the conclusion that companies they work for provide life insurance programs at cheap flat rates. You may even do this to leave extra money for your kids. "You may be surprised if you price it out that the rates often are more expensive then what you can get on an individual policy if you're in good health," cautions Sackler. Before buying, find out the price of an individual policy. The individual policy may also give you guaranteed insurability (i.e., renewals) in future years, which can be important. Finally, before buying any insurance, ask your lawyer whether it should be in a trust. This can avoid taxes and protect the proceeds.

Here's how a typical poorly planned divorce agreement can play out. Suppose you are required to keep $500,000 of life insurance for your ex for 15 years. If you die after remarrying, your ex gets the required $500,000. But because you owned the policy, it's taxed in your estate. Who pays the tax? Your new wife? You probably will have assured a tax and legal nightmare for your heirs. See an estate planner and get it straightened out while you're above ground.

Sidney Kess, a New York City attorney and CPA, demonstrates the problems that can be caused by failing to change beneficiary designations. Kess described a divorce where the husband was an IRS enrolled agent, so he was certainly smart enough to understand the importance of beneficiary designations. After the divorce, the wife remarried, and her former husband was so distraught that he committed suicide. There were two children from the earlier marriage. They went to their mother and explained that their dad had told them that he wanted the insurance money for their education. The wife, enjoying her new life, told her own kids to "drop dead." The children, realizing that they might not be able to go to college without the insurance money, hired an attorney and sued their mother for the insurance money based only on their knowledge that their dad had wanted to change the beneficiary of the insurance to them. The court held "no go!" Mom was entitled to the insurance money because the insurance was a contract, and the contract clearly listed her as the recipient. "So change your papers when you complete the divorce. Get your beneficiary designation right!" cautions Sidney Kess.

Rule #149. Make Sure You Control Access to Your Safe Deposit Box

Whose name is on your safe deposit box? The contents probably have already been dealt with in the divorce, but don't forget to change the authorized signers. Have your ex-wife's name removed. Better yet, if a new box is available in the bank, just take out a new box and avoid any issues of access to the old one.

Safe deposit boxes can be important. Now that you're single, tell someone you can rely on in an emergency where the box is and the number. Make sure your bank knows this person can have access in an emergency. Here's a checklist of documents you should store in the box:

- ✔ Birth certificate.

- ✔ Passport (who has the kids' passports?).

- ✔ Photos of key assets and of your new home (in case of fire or theft).

- ✔ Copy of your will.

- ✔ Extra durable powers of attorney (not naming your ex).

- ✔ Valuables (especially if you're still relocating).

- ✔ Real estate deed.

- ✔ Other important original legal documents.

If any of these have been misplaced during the divorce and moving out of your former home, get new documents. Keep copies at your new home.

11

Handling Legal, Financial, and Other Problems That Don't End with the Divorce

Rule #150. Know Your Rights If Your Ex Violates Your Divorce Agreement

"In the real world, the agreement is only as good as the people who perform it. The real teeth is the parties respecting the order. Privately agreed upon solutions have a much higher level of success than court-imposed solutions," says Barry Croland, Esq., Shapiro & Croland, Hackensack, New Jersey. The moral is simple; try to work out an agreement that you can both live with and don't rely on court enforcement. Anytime an issue arises for which a modification of the agreement may even be appropriate, you still have to address whether the costs of modification and the emotional difficulties it will revive are worth the possible benefit.

Rule #151. Protect Your Finances If You Remarry to Minimize Your Ex-Wife's Re-petitioning the Court

If you remarry and your new wife has income and assets, what should you do?

Try to keep your assets separate from those of your new spouse, and get a prenuptial agreement. This protects both you and your new wife. For example, in Tennessee, your ex-wife can subpoena your new wife's tax records if you have a joint account with your new wife. Your ex-wife can use this financial information to see if your new wife is contributing to your household expenses, which minimizes your current expenses, thus potentially freeing up more money for your ex-wife. The more money you have available, the more you may have to pay in child support to your ex-wife. In Tennessee, the courts only look at what you earn; other states use a shared-income approach, looking at earnings of your new wife as well, cautions Amy J. Amundsen, Esq., of Memphis, Tennessee.

In Connecticut, although your new wife's salary can't be considered if your first wife re-petitions, your new wife's payment of expenses can be a factor.

Rule #152. Find Out If Your Ex Is Cohabiting

If your ex-wife is cohabiting and you can demonstrate that her partner is covering some portion of her living expenses, you might be able to petition the court to reduce your alimony obligations. The task won't be easy. You'll have to prove the cohabitation and demonstrate the coverage of expenses when you may have little or no access to any records of her partner.

Rule #153. Don't Give the Court Any Information That Is Not Specifically Required

In some states you have to provide financial data to the court on an annual basis. The rules may require you to provide an income report to the court, including your tax return. This information may then be sent to your ex for her to determine whether she wants to try to increase the alimony or child support you pay. Some states might then automatically increase child support based on your increases in income. Carefully review your state's requirements to determine what, if anything, you can do to minimize your risks, warns Amundsen.

Rule #154. Try to Prevent Your Ex from Moving with the Kids out of State

If you want to oppose your ex moving with your children out of state, consider the following:

✔ Evaluate each reason she gives for the move and make her demonstrate that they are reasonable.

✔ Try to find out her real motive. If she claims that it is for a job opportunity, make sure she demonstrates that there are insufficient job opportunities locally. Also, make sure she factors the cost of living and moving costs into the economic analysis.

✔ Ask your ex-wife to corroborate the emotional and personal advantages for the children from the move. Has she really demonstrated that the move will be in the best interest of the children? How? Examine the basis of her claims and whether local benefits have been properly evaluated.

✔ Protect your visitation rights and other access to the children. Are the children old and mature enough to travel on their own to visit you?

✔ If you had a nonmove provision in the divorce agreement, ask your lawyer to enforce it.

Rule #155. Protect Yourself If You Need to File for Bankruptcy

Occasionally, a state court may consider your bankruptcy to be a cause for a change in circumstances and may modify your divorce decree, says Colleen A. Brown, Esq., of Lawrence, Werner, Kesselring, Swartout & Brown, LLP, Canandaigua, New York. As a result of your bankruptcy, you may have no debt and your ex-wife may have substantial debt. If you declare bankruptcy and you're released in bankruptcy from your debts, the court may modify your divorce agreement and require you to pay greater child support and alimony if the original divorce settlement was based on your debt payments. Now, as a result of your bankruptcy, your ex-wife may have to pay joint debts, so you may lose out in any event. Other courts won't do this because of the "supremacy clause" of the United States Constitution which provides that state courts must defer to federal bankruptcy court. If your ex-wife tries to go back to court to argue for an increase in alimony and child support as a result of your discharge of debts in your bankruptcy, ask your lawyer to argue against this on the basis that a modification would undue what the bankruptcy was to accomplish. A modification would undermine the fresh start you are supposed to get as a result of the bankruptcy process, suggests Brown.

Rule #156. Understand How Your Bankruptcy Could Help You

You may be required to pay your ex-wife maintenance but obfuscate the language in your agreement to make it sound like a property settlement, because support obligations (i.e., alimony, maintenance, child support) cannot be discharged in bankruptcy, but a property settlement can be. So if you declare bankruptcy, you would prefer that your divorce agreement had been couched in terms of a property transfer, not a maintenance payment. Keeping a roof over your spouse and children is considered support. Distributions from your company, if your ex-wife is no longer an owner, may be considered property by the bankruptcy court. Different courts have different standards; just make sure the agreement is clear as to whether a particular obligation you have is a property transfer or a support payment. Thus, in some situations obfuscation may be an affirmative planning tool. Certainly, if the agreement is not clear and you have to declare bankruptcy, ask your attorney to argue that your obligations should be discharged as a property settlement. But keep in mind that if your agreement is not clear, the bankruptcy court may have an evidentiary hearing to establish what the parties intended, which is not only not fun but very expensive.

The bankruptcy court can characterize a distribution of assets differently than the matrimonial documents did. For tax reasons, you may try to treat a payment as maintenance so it's deductible. Thus, you may say in the divorce agreement that $500 per month for five years is maintenance. The court may look at this agreement and decide that it's not maintenance, but rather, it's a property distribution. And as a property distribution, your obligation can be wiped out in bankruptcy forever.

Support arrears are not discharged in bankruptcy and must be paid. If you file bankruptcy under Chapter 13 and the plan provides that you are to pay off your creditors over three to five years, you will also continue to pay your ex-wife any property settlement remaining through the bankruptcy plan over the same time period based on your pro rata share. If all your creditors get 30 percent, your ex-wife will get her 30 percent at the same time. Chapter 7 bankruptcy is an instant discharge, so your ex-wife can go after your wages the day after you file, notes Colleen Brown.

Rule #157. Understand How Your Ex-wife's Bankruptcy Can Hurt You

If your ex-wife files for bankruptcy, pay attention. Have your attorney review the schedules your wife files with the bankruptcy court to make sure all assets are listed and find out how her bankruptcy affects your financial situation. The best place for trustees to get dirt on fraud by a debtor in bankruptcy is from an ex-spouse: it's amazing how many people forget about their boat in storage, the antique jewelry in the attic, and so on. If the trustee finds out that there is money to pay, they will pursue it. You want to make sure that all your ex-wife's assets are reported so you don't get saddled with her debt later.

Rule #158. Join a Support Group

Consider joining a support group for divorced dads. Read a lot and be informed. You have to take primary responsibility for maintaining the relationships with your children. Society won't generally help you. Society pushes parents away from their children by making parents litigate to maintain a relationship with their children, says David L. Levy, Esq., President and cofounder, Children's Rights Council, in Washington, D.C.

CONCLUSION

Divorce is one of life's most traumatic emotional experiences. Unfortunately, the myriad of complex technical issues such as taxes, valuations, legal entanglements, and more, only exacerbate the personal difficulties. While there are many professionals who can make the process easier, less costly, and even less painful, it is not always simple to identify which type of professional you should consult for each issue, and even more difficult to ferret out capable professionals. The bottom line is you have to be your own advocate. While you may not understand all the technical nuances of each issue, you must understand the broad strokes—the big picture. You must take an active role in hiring and monitoring the professionals you work with. The more organized your records, the better you document each item in writing, the better result you are likely to achieve.

Throughout the process, especially if children are involved, you'll have to grit your teeth and push forward. Many aspects of the "system" are unfair to men. In spite of all the political correctness, equality in many important areas has simply not occurred. Even favorable changes in the law cannot assure that attitudes favoring women in access to children and other important areas have changed. There is no easy answer, but applying the many tips in this book, and avoiding as many of the pitfalls this book has warned you about, will improve the likelihood of a fairer result and a less costly settlement, and enable you to more quickly get on with your life. This book has not stoked your hatred and has not given you "dirty tricks" to play. Although so very many divorce books for men focus on these approaches, they just don't work.

Good luck.

RECOMMENDED READING
AND ADDITIONAL SOURCES
OF INFORMATION

The web site *www.laweasy.com* provides extensive information, legal tips, and sample documents.

For more information on estate planning and divorce, see Martin M. Shenkman, *The Complete Book of Trusts,* 2nd edition (New York: John Wiley & Sons, Inc., 1999).

For more information and templates to use for creating budgets and organizing finances, see Martin M. Shenkman, *The Beneficiary Workbook* (New York: John Wiley & Sons, Inc., 1999).

The Tax Practitioner's Guide to Reviewing Legal Documents, by Martin M. Shenkman, Practitioners Publishing Company, 800-323-8724 (available 2001).

For information on Jewish issues and divorce contact Kayama 800-932-8589, www.kayama.org.

Matrimonial Strategist newsletter. Call 212-545-6184 for more information.

INDEX

Index

Index

Index

Index

Index

Illegality, avoiding, 6
Information disclosure. *See*
   Disclosure
Inheritance, disclaiming, 42
In-laws, staying on good terms with,
   54
Insurance buyout agreement, 136
Insurance coverage:
   business, 136–137
   during divorce process, 119–120
   reviewing after divorce, 206–208
Investment strategies, reviewing, 204
IRA (individual retirement account).
   See Retirement assets

Joint-and-survivor annuity, 129
Joint bank accounts, 38
Joint custody arrangements:
   legal custody, 69–70
   tax deduction for dependent(s),
      180–181
Joint debts, 140–141
Joint income tax return, 182
Joint liability problem, credit cards,
   49

Kess, Sidney, 125, 126, 128, 129,
   171, 174, 208
Kiddie tax, 104

Laweasy.com, 223
Lawyer(s), 19, 21–42
   gathering information for, 27–30
   getting file from, when divorce
      finalized, 37
   hiring, *vs.* not hiring, 23–25
   interviewing thoroughly, 26–27
   making sure wife has proper legal/
      financial representation,
      33–34

not paying from your business,
   167–168
picking right lawyer for your case,
   24–25
questions to ask before hiring,
   26–27
remaining boss of "wiggle-room"
   in the law, 30–32
wife's, 27, 31
Leasing assets (cars/computers),
   205
Leitman, David, 109
Levy, David L., 31, 70, 71, 219
Life after divorce. *See* Postdivorce
   issues
Life insurance policies, reevaluating,
   207–208
Liquidity (key postdivorce financial
   objective), 205
Living wills/trust, 39, 40
Loan (using to equalize hard-to-
   divide assets), 117

Mail (obtaining post office box),
   54–55
Mareva injunction, 109
Marital assets. *See* Assets
Marital residence. *See* House
   (marital residence)
Marital status, tax reporting
   purposes, 183–184
Marriage, state of (being decisive
   about), 3
Mediation, 4, 19, 30, 34–37, 47
Medical emergencies, 101
Medical insurance, 119–120, 206
Moving:
   ex-wife's moving out of state with
      children, 215
   getting post office box, 54–55

Index

Index

Index

Index